Caliphates and Islamic Global Politics

EDITED BY

TIMOTHY POIRSON AND ROBERT OPRISKO

E-INTERNATIONAL RELATIONS PUBLISHING

E-IR Edited Collections
Series Editors: Stephen McGlinchey, Marianna Karakoulaki and Robert L. Oprisko

E-IR's Edited Collections are open access scholarly books presented in a format that preferences brevity and accessibility while retaining academic conventions. Each book is available in print and e-book, and is published under a Creative Commons CC BY-NC 4.0 license. As E-International Relations is committed to open access in the fullest sense, free electronic versions of all of our books, including this one, are available on the E-International Relations website.

Find out more at: http://www.e-ir.info/publications

Recent titles
Nations under God: The Geopolitics of Faith in the Twenty-first Century

Popular Culture and World Politics: Theories, Methods, Pedagogies

Ukraine and Russia: People, Politics, Propaganda and Perspectives

Forthcoming
System, Society & the World: Exploring the English School (2nd Edition)

Environment, Climate Change and International Relations: Tendencies, Assessments and Perspectives.

About the E-International Relations website
E-International Relations (www.E-IR.info) is the world's leading open access website for students and scholars of international politics. E-IR's daily publications feature expert articles, blogs, reviews and interviews – as well as a range of high quality student contributions. The website was established in November 2007 and now reaches over 200,000 unique visitors a month. E-IR is run by a registered non-profit organisation based in Bristol, England and staffed with an all-volunteer team.

E-International Relations
www.E-IR.info
Bristol, England
Published 2014 (e-book), 2015 (print)

This book is published under a Creative Commons CC BY-NC 4.0 license. You are free to:

- **Share** — copy and redistribute the material in any medium or format.
- **Adapt** — remix, transform, and build upon the material.

Under the following terms:

- **Attribution** — You must give appropriate credit, provide a link to the license, and indicate if changes were made. You may do so in any reasonable manner, but not in any way that suggests the licensor endorses you or your use.
- **NonCommercial** — You may not use the material for commercial purposes.

Any of the above conditions can be waived if you get permission. Please contact info@e-ir.info for any such enquiries.

Other than the license terms noted above, there are no restrictions placed on the use and dissemination of this book for student learning materials / scholarly use.

Copy Editing: Michael Pang
Production: Ran Xiao and Michael Tang

Cover Image: Javarman (Konstantin Kalishko)

ISBN 978-1-910814-10-9

A catalogue record for this book is available from the British Library.

Acknowledgements

The editor would like to thank, first and foremost, the contributors to this volume, whose hard work and dedication, and willingness to engage with the topic at large, made this possible.

On a more personal note, I would like to thank Dr. Robert L. Oprisko and Dr. Stephen McGlinchey.

Robert, thank you for your help, advice, and mentorship ... and for coming up with the title of the collection, which I kept as it was too well phrased to not put out there! Thank you for mentoring me through this.

Stephen, thank you for being such an attentive Editor-in-chief, and for your patience despite my many emails regarding my uncertainties. Thank you for pushing this forward and making sure I stuck to it despite certain setbacks, and for giving me the opportunity to commission this collection and publish it with E-International Relations.

Timothy Poirson, Editor

Abstract

The events of the 2011 Arab Spring saw renewed hope for Arab Civil Society, at least in the eyes of Middle East observers. However, with the cases of Libya and Syria descending into civil war and chaos, and the Egyptian military still holding the country in a tight grip, the success of Civil Society at creating a space for itself is questionable. While the fall of seemingly immovable authoritarian regimes did not seem to profit much to Civil Society, Political Islamic movements took advantage of the vacuum to establish their bases and launch operations to implement their ideology. Two to three years after the first Uprisings, Islamist groups are making a strong comeback in certain Middle East/North African countries. In Syria, Iraq, towns in Libya, and a town in Lebanon, groups like the Islamic State or Ansar al-Sharia are declaring Caliphates in the territories they seize, in an attempt to fulfil the Political Islam ideal of a 'global Islamic Caliphate' encompassing the entirety of the Muslim world. This edited collection aims to address common questions about Political Islam, as well as to provide an assessment of ISIS and finally challenge common understandings on the issue of Islam and democracy.

Timothy Poirson is a PhD candidate at the School of International Relations/Handa Centre for the Study of Terrorism and Political Violence at the University of Saint Andrews. He holds a bachelor's degree from the Paris Institute of Political Science (Sciences Po Paris) and an MLitt (Master of Letters) in Peace and Conflict Studies from the University of Saint Andrews. His PhD thesis and the bulk of his work revolves around post-Arab Spring Libya. His other areas of research include Political Islam, Civil Society in a post-Colonial theoretical framework, as well as the Middle East and its politics. He can be contacted at tmp@st-andrews.ac.uk and followed online on his Academia.edu profile.

Robert L. Oprisko is a research fellow at Indiana University's Center for the Study of Global Change, as well as Editor-at-large of E-International Relations and a Director of the website's Editorial Board. His research focuses on contemporary political philosophy, international relations theory, and critical university studies. His books include Honor: A Phenomenology (Routledge, 2012) and Michael A. Weinstein: Action, Contemplation, Vitalism (Routledge, 2014).

Contents

INTRODUCTION
Timothy Poirson　　1

1. ISLAMIC STATE, THE ARAB SPRING, AND THE DISENCHANTMENT WITH POLITICAL ISLAM
Maximilian Lakitsch　　6

2. IMAMATE AND CALIPHATE: ISLAMIC GOVERNANCE THEORY IN MOROCCAN ISLAMIST DISCOURSE
Juan A. Macías-Amoretti　　16

3. LEGAL PLURALISM AND SHARIA: IMPLEMENTING ISLAMIC LAW IN STATES AND SOCIETIES
Adel Elsayed Sparr　　24

4. COMPARING GOALS AND ASPIRATIONS OF NATIONAL VS. TRANSNATIONAL ISLAMIST MOVEMENTS
Joseph Kaminski　　35

5. THE ISLAMIC STATE AND THE ARAB TRIBES IN EASTERN SYRIA
Haian Dukhan and Sinan Hawat　　49

6. BEYOND ARMS AND BEARDS: LOCAL GOVERNANCE OF ISIS IN SYRIA
Rana Khalaf　　57

7. THE ISLAMIC STATE AND ITS VIABILITY
Mohammed Nuruzzaman　　68

8. WHAT IS ISLAMIC DEMOCRACY? THE THREE CS OF ISLAMIC GOVERNANCE
M. A. Muqtedar Khan　　79

CONTRIBUTORS　　86
NOTE ON INDEXING　　88

Introduction

Caliphates and Islamic Global Politics

TIMOTHY POIRSON
UNIVERSITY OF SAINT ANDREWS, SCOTLAND (UK)

As the year 2014 is slowly drawing to a close, we begin to look back with an attempt to understand why and how certain events happened. Islamist political groups enjoyed a strong surge of advancement in certain Middle Eastern/North African countries. They now represent an important type of non-state actors in contemporary international relations. Groups like Islamic State or Ansar al-Sharia are declaring caliphates in the territories they seize, which challenges the sovereignty of established states like Syria, Libya, Iraq, and Lebanon. Who are these groups? What prompted their creation, and on what grounds do they operate? What real threat do they pose to regional stability and to the international community?

Political Islam is a term that is often used amongst circles of academics and policymakers, but its complexity is seldom acknowledged or understood. 'Political Islamic movements' believe that Islam has a built-in political system that every believer should adhere to and uphold (Khan, 2014). Islamist groups are motivated by the idea that there is "not enough Islam" in society (Woltering, 2002:1133). There can be no 'Islamisation' of society until an Islamic political system replaces the existing one. The path to reach said 'Islamisation' varies according to which group is operating and their specific circumstances, however, the implementation of sharia is a tool that is commonly held and for which is popularly advocated (Woltering, 2002:1133). In the wake of the heightening of Islamist activity in the Middle East and North Africa (MENA), particularly with the rise to pre-eminence of the Islamic State – also known as Islamic State in Iraq and Syria (ISIS), Islamic State in Iraq and the Levantine (ISIL), or by the Arabic acronym Daesh – questions about this misunderstood legal tradition have been posed by Western media and policymakers, oftentimes demonstrating little understanding of the historical wealth and implications of this tradition.

Following the 9/11 attacks, the threat of communism has seemingly been replaced by the fear of Islam in the Western World. It is seen as both a 'major threat' to Western democracies and its civil society, but also to Arab civil societies (Turam, 2004:259). Academic literature on the perception of contemporary Political Islamic movements, however, is polarised. On one side are scholars who see Islam as the staunch enemy of liberal democracy and civil society (Gellner, 1996; Huntington, 1996). On the other, political Islam is portrayed as a 'propellant' of civil society by embodying the only strong opposition voice in the sea of repressive authoritarian regimes in the Arab World (Hefner, 2000; Norton, 1995). The latter voices construct their argument on the idea that, despite being a notion plagued by definitional issues, civil society is pitted as a platform for criticism of the State (Turam, 2004:260), which is the same assumption as Islamist groups, who, beyond a simple criticism of the State, possess a 'secularisation-resistant' essence (Gellner, 1996:15) that struggles with the State. Having said that, many Middle East observers contest the idea of an Arab civil society. Indeed, these observers argue that it has been absent, or at the very least stunted, in development for centuries.

The Arab pre-modern society was initially centred around a political authority whose legitimacy rested upon a combination of conquest and religious doctrine. It included a public space shared by merchants, guilds, and Sufi orders (Gellner, 1988). Outwith this political authority, other collectivities operated in an autonomous and defiant manner, mainly tribal and ethnic groups who ran their own internal affairs through 'elected or appointed leaders' (Ibrahim, 1998:375). Overall, traditional forms of authority embodied by leaders, elders, and elites were performing the functions that provided the governance of these societies. Social solidarities existed along multiple lines, such as religious and ethnic ones (Ibrahim, 1998:376-377). Its socio-political structure changed considerably following the colonial era in the 19th and early 20th century. New Arab states were born, carved into existence by externally dictated artificial borders. In addition to this, these new states initially ignored pre-modern era traditional wisdom (Ibrahim, 1998:377) when building their institutions, resulting in society being kept passive through paternalistic authoritarian regimes that kept society in the dark, away from decision-making circles.

Despite the repressive nature of the governmental authorities in the post-World War One MENA states, Islamist groups started to appear as early as the late 1920s with the Egyptian Muslim Brotherhood. Such groups developed as strong movements in opposition to repressive government, sometimes even posing serious security threats to the regime. Often, the governmental response was to increase draconian measures to silence Islamist groups, which were ineffective at eliminating these groups as a challenge, and intensified public support. During the 1980s and the 1990s, MENA civil society found itself caught in a struggle between authoritarian regimes and

Islamist groups, going so far as having some members of this civil society drawn into these Islamist groups, or else silenced (Ibrahim, 1998:378).

The events of the 2011 Arab Spring saw renewed hope for Arab civil society, at least in the eyes of Middle East observers. This optimism was tempered, however, when the protest-driven democratic movements encountered resistance (Oprisko, 2013). Libya and Syria descended into civil war, and the Egyptian military overthrew Mohammed Morsi, the democratically elected president and member of the Muslim Brotherhood. The success of civil society at creating a space for itself remains questionable. While the fall of seemingly immovable authoritarian regimes did not seem to profit much to civil society, it has been Political Islamist movements, rather than civil society, which have taken advantage of the power vacuum following the Arab Spring movements. These successes are evident in both Libya and Syria, where ISIS and ISIL have carved out territory in which to establish bases to launch operations and in which to implement their ideology and consolidate power. Groups like Islamic State or Ansar al-Sharia are declaring Caliphates in the territories they seize, in an attempt to fulfil the Political Islam ideal of a 'global Islamic Caliphate'. Political Islam is thus perceived as representing a clear and present danger to the liberal international order and its current status quo because it is a competitive vision for how the world ought to be ordered.

The broad scope of this direct challenge is what prompted the creation of this edited collection. The goal herein is to provide greater understanding of contemporary 'radical' political Islamic activism, illuminating the new trends set by ISIS or Ansar al-Sharia, in how Islamist movements operate. It aims to make the reader think beyond the media headlines and consider the realities of such caliphates proclaimed by these groups. This collection also aims to offer a perspective on what the implications for world politics are.

To this effect, we have included eight contributions on caliphates and their impact on international politics. Maximilian Lakitsch opens the conversation with his article titled 'Islamic State, the Arab Spring, and the Disenchantment with Political Islam', providing a broad view of the major themes broached throughout the entire collection: Political Islam, the Islamic State, and the new role of Political Islam in the Middle East.

Juan A. Macías-Amoretti contributes the next article of this volume, 'Imamate and Caliphate, Islamic Governance Theory in Moroccan Islamist Discourse', which examines Islamic theory on governance, using Morocco as a case study to analyse the concepts of the 'caliphate' and 'imamate' in Moroccan Islamic political discourse.

Moving from governance to legal doctrine, Adel Elsayed Sparr, in his article titled 'Legal Pluralism and Sharia: Implementing Islamic Law in States and Societies', sheds light on Sharia's applicability in States and societies. He looks at the role it plays in today's societies, and the role and potential is does and should have. Elsayed Sparr concludes that the debate is not about the religious will of God, but instead about the political will of the people and their representation under an equal citizenship.

Joseph J. Kaminski makes a compelling case that national-based Islamist movements make more of a compelling effort to be recognised as legitimate political actors by the rest of the world. He argues that they adopt a more moderate and inclusion-centric discourse, which is something transnational Islamist movements care little about. His comparative analysis of contemporary national-based and transnational-based Islamist movements, which focuses on differences and similarities in goals and aspirations, follows Elsayed Sparr's article.

The next three articles that follow adopt a case-specific angle, that of the Islamic State and its presence in Syria. Haian Dukhan and Sinan al-Hawat examine the relationship between the Islamic State and the Arab tribes in Eastern Syria, arguing that shared economic and political interests, as well as common enemies, facilitate the group's building of a relationship with the tribal communities in Syria. This article ends by concluding that the longer the Islamic State remains in control of large portions of the Syrian territory, the deeper the relationship between the tribes and the group will be, and the harder it will be for external actors to fight the group militarily and ideologically. Rana Khalaf illuminates the Islamic State's local governance in Syria, and analyses the interactions between the group and civil society, where the group clearly dominates a weak and seemingly powerless Syria. The penultimate article of this collection, authored by Mohammed Nuruzzaman, explores the political, military, and economic viability of the Islamic State.

Wrapping up this edited collection is M.A. Muqtedar Khan's article presenting the 'Three Cs of Islamic Governance'. Posing the question of 'What is Islamic Democracy?', Khan concludes there are many elements in Islamic tradition that make Islam a facilitator – rather than a barrier – to democracy, justice, and tolerance in the Muslim World. This serves to raise the debate on Political Islam, and put perspective on the mainstream view that Islam and democracy – because of the nature of certain Islamist movements – are not compatible, by going back to an analysis of the Quran and Sharia.

References

Gellner, E. Plough, *Sword and Book: The Structure of Human Society.* London:Collins (1988)

Gellner, E. *Conditions of Liberty: Civil Society and Its Rivals.* Penguin (1996)

Huntington, S.P. *The Clash of Civilisation and the Remaking of World Order.* New York:Touchstone (1996)

Ibrahim, S.E. "The Troubled Triangle: Populism, Islam, and Civil Society in the Arab World." *International Political Science Review* (1998).

Oprisko, R.L. "Egypt's Three-Card Monte: The Arab Spring and Human Revolution." *E-International Relations* (2013). Published electronically July 23, 2013. http://www.e-ir.info/2013/07/23/egypts-three-card-monte-the-arab-spring-and-human-revolution/.

Woltering, Robbert A.F.L. "The Roots of Islamist Popularity." *Third World Quarterly* (2002).

Turam, B. "The Politics of Engagement between Islam and the Secular State: Ambivalences of 'Civil Society'." *The British Journal of Sociology* (2004).

1

Islamic State, the Arab Spring, and the Disenchantment with Political Islam

MAXIMILIAN LAKITSCH
AUSTRIAN CENTRE FOR PEACE AND CONFLICT RESOLUTION

Egypt's Muslim Brotherhood being supported by a large part of the population despite the strong government repression it exercises, Islamist Militia haunting a barely existing central government in Libya, and various Jihadi groups playing a crucial role in the Syrian civil war all seem to be closely related to Political Islam. Above all, it is the sudden and strong presence of Islamic State (IS) in Iraq and Syria which adds most to the impression of a new era of dominance of Political Islam. However, developments like the success of the social protests in North Africa in ousting their autocratic governments, as well as the image of Islamist militia in Libya, Syria, and Iraq as being sectarian and self-serving actors, may have brought about disenchantment with Political Islam as a means for social and political justice. That being the case, Political Islam may face a significant decline in influencing national, regional, and global events in the near future.

The traditional foundations of Political Islam

Islam already has political implications within its foundations. However, what is commonly understood as Political Islam and its synonym 'Islamism' is a specific modern interpretation of Islam. It has its roots in social conflicts: the establishment of autocratic monarchies in the newly independent Arab countries in the 1950s and 1960s gave rise to social justice demands which these regimes did not meet (Hourani 2005: 373-458). The population had two available means of expressing their discontent.

The first one is the ideology of modern Political Islam. From the late 19th century until the second half of the 20th century, scholars such as Jamal al-Afghani, Muhammad Abduh, Abul Ala Maududi, and Sayyid Qutb prescribed a fundamental re-interpretation of Islam as a genuine base of empowered Arab societies in the face of Western imperialism – Islam is the solution to political and social problems (al-Din al-Afghani 2003; Abduh 1966; al-Maududi 1955; Qutb 2007).

The second one is the ideology of Arab Socialism. Intellectuals like Michel Aflaq and Salah al-Din al-Bitar developed an Arab adaption of traditional socialist ideas as a genuine foundation of Arab societies in order to face political and social demands for power and justice against imperialism and capitalism. The Baath party, for instance, subsequently became one of the most influential organisations, with Egyptian president Gamal Abdel Nasser as Arab Socialism's most influential proponent (al-Husri 1976; Dawisa 2005).

Arab Socialism became dominant all over North Africa and the Middle East. As an egalitarian ideology, it was attractive both for the general population, but also specifically for young and ambitious men from poorer families, who often sought to climb the social ladder through an army career as an officer. As a consequence, young officers who claimed to represent the cause of Arab Socialism led various military coup d'états against the monarchies. That was the case in Iraq, Syria, and Egypt. In Algeria, Arab Socialism came into power with the achievement of independence under the lead of the socialist Front de Libération Nationale (FLN). For Palestinians, Fatah's socialist ideology was undisputed (Hourani 2005: 401-415; Fisk 2006: 181-183).

However, throughout the years, these socialist leaders and parties were not only unable to meet their populations' demands, but they also grew more and more autocratic. As their legitimacy decreased, the regimes depended more and more on a vast network of intelligence agencies, which had to deeply penetrate society. Socialist Arab states became so called mukhabarat (Arabic for "intelligence") states. Since societies were closely monitored and public opinions about social and political issues were forbidden, the only remaining and available means of expressing discontent, apart from discredited Arab Socialism, was Political Islam. Political Islam became the monopoly of expressing social and political discontent. The hope of fulfilling political and social justice demands was predominantly linked to Political Islam: the Muslim Brotherhood in Egypt, Syria, and Jordan; Hamas in Palestine; Front Islamique du Salut (FIS) in Algeria; but also al-Qaeda, as the armed pan-Arab actor pursuing the cause of Political Islam through Jihad. From 1970 onwards, those parties and groups grew increasingly popular, and with it their ability to influence the political and social agenda on a national, regional, and global level. Thus, Political Islam inherited the monopoly of expression (Kepel 2002: 43-105).

In the last few years, the influence of Political Islam in global politics was perceived to have grown from the aftermath of the Arab Spring, as well as due to the military strength of Islamic State in Iraq and Syria. However, at the same time, these developments may also indicate certain reconfigurations of Political Islam, which have actually eroded its traditional foundations and therefore may lead to its decline.

Re-thinking the Arab State

On December 17, 2010, thousands of Tunisians spontaneously took to the streets to protests against their government following the self-immolation of young Mohamed Bouazizi. The successful ouster of autocratic president Zine el-Abidine Ben Ali by the mass protests led people in Egypt to protest against Hosni Mubarak. Both of those manifestations of public indignation overthrew a dictator. Both of those protest movements effectively dealt with their source of indignation – they were successful. Following these events, a collective feeling of relief swept through North Africa and the Middle East that individuals can raise their demands peacefully beyond any party or ideology, and can thereby succeed against an almighty state. In other words, the successful protests in Egypt and Tunisia provided people in North Africa and the Middle East with a new means of expressing their discontent in the face of the state: civic public protest. Thus, the political paradigm shifted to a modern one; it is not the citizen who serves the state, but the citizen is the actual raison d'être of the state.

However, as mass demonstrations in Libya and Syria led to civil wars, the original momentum of political hope, which had been labeled the Arab Spring, was already being suspected as a delusion. Although the political developments in Tunisia in 2014 turned out to be favorable for most of the population, they were overshadowed by certain political disillusion. Firstly, mass protests in Libya and Yemen[1] were perceived as manifestations of an emerging civil society, whereas they should have better been treated as particular sectarian or regional interests. Thus, the protests in Yemen succeeded in nothing but changing their leaders' names; protests in Libya led to the disintegration of Libya and the emergence of dozens of predominantly Islamist militias. Furthermore, protests in Syria led to a full-blown war. As the war continues, the situation becomes more and more unmanageable, and the original social conflict transformed into a battleground for various armed factions, which are dominantly foreign as well as Islamist and have other goals than a better future for Syria. Finally, the ouster of newly elected president Mohamed Morsi of the Muslim Brotherhood due to autocratic tendencies[2], and his replacement by the military's supreme leader Abdel Fatah as-Sisi, gave the impression that what was emphatically an Arab Spring was just an unsuccessful experiment of liberty which was doomed to fail anyway.

Consequently, it might seem that we are witnessing the legacy of an "Arab Winter" (Spencer 2012; Spencer 2014) or an "Islamist Spring" (Dergham 2012), rather than being able to draw any positive conclusions about the region's political future. Nevertheless, it is the protest movements in Tunisia and Egypt which have already reconfigured the political foundations in a way that does not favour Political Islam: they have provided the MENA with a new paradigm for raising political and social demands through simple civic means. This stretches beyond any ethnic or religious affiliation, and beyond from Arab Socialism and Political Islam. Those protests provided the people with a whole new ideological space which not only transcended political, religious, and ethnic affiliations, but also opened a whole new set of ideas waiting to aggravate and be expressed. Thus, one important legacy of the Arab Spring is a first glimpse of something like an Arab civil society.

The Arab Spring even reached war-torn Algeria. Having gone through an enormously long and brutal war of liberation, as well as a very bloody civil war in the 1990s, the country seemed to be fed up with revolutions (Fisk 2006: 631-719). At the same time, Algeria seemed to be more than ripe for a revolution after decades of autocratic reign of the Front de Libération Nationale (FLN). Whereas the country's elite profited from the enormous amount of natural resources, it did not respond to the demands of its enormously poor population. Consequently, after witnessing its neighbours succeed in getting rid of their dictators, some mass demonstrations took place from 2010 to 2012, which were brutally repressed by the regime ('Algeria' 2012). Nevertheless, when the old and critically ill president Abdel Aziz Bouteflika was declared newly elected president for a fourth term in 2014, there were again cautious expressions of public indignation. Unlike in the 1980s and 1990s, it is not Political Islam which seems to benefit from this political indignation, but also protest movements like Barakat (Algerian Arabic for "enough") being founded. This thus begins to indicate an emerging civil society (Mouloudj 2014).

Islamic State and Political Islam's self-interest

Mass protests in Benghazi and the following ouster of Muammar Gaddafi led to the social and political disintegration of Libya. This vacuum became a new hotspot of global Jihad[3]. In Syria, Al-Nusra Front and the Islamic State of Iraq and al-Sham (ISIS) became the two main Islamist militia groups fighting Bashar al-Assad's regime. ISIS occupied large parts of Eastern Syria in 2013, in addition to its already captured territory in Western Iraq. Thus, ISIS's occupied areas already looked like territory for a new state between Syria and Iraq. Finally, in June 2014, ISIS launched a full-scale offensive in Iraq, which led to the sudden and successful seizing of very large areas of Iraq. Following this, ISIS dropped two letters from its acronym and became Islamic State (IS). The fall of Baghdad was believed to be only a matter of time.

Although it might look like Political Islam has entered a higher stage of existence by becoming an unstoppable military and political force, this very transformation has actually again eroded Political Islam's foundations leading to its loss of influence and power. Three developments are fuelling this reconfiguration. Firstly, IS is exercising power in its territories in a very cruel way by killing thousands of people, often randomly. It has nearly no legitimacy in its conquered territories (Weber 1978: 212-215). Secondly, in Syria, IS first sided with the al-Nusra Front and the secular Free Syrian Army (FSA) against the regime. However, power struggles between al-Nusra and IS led to fighting, which caused more than 4,000 deaths so far. That opened a new front: FSA and al-Nusra against IS. Consequently, IS is more and more perceived as an ordinary militia group following its own power ambitions, rather than representing the Islamic answer to the peoples' social and political demands. Finally, IS is fundamentally sectarian. It tends to consider everything but Sunni Islam as infidelity. Abu Musab al-Zarqawi, a crucial predecessor of current leader Abu Omar al-Baghdadi, had initiated Jihad in Iraq in 2003, and declared war on Shia Muslims in 2005 ('al-Zarqawi declares war on Iraqi Shia' 2005). Although there might be some tensions and mistrust between Sunni and Shia believers throughout the MENA, declaring Sunni or Shia a target in Jihad is barely supported in those countries.

Nuri al-Maliki's sectarian politics in Iraq and the discrimination of the Sunni population were the major shift which allowed the Sunni militia IS to conquer vast parts of Iraq. As a matter of fact, local support in Iraq is or was because of sectarian politics. The peaceful power shift to Haider al-Abadi, who promised inclusive politics, is already backed by Sunni leaders and clerics. So IS is very likely to lose its local support again. IS will again be what it was from the beginning: an actor whose strength does not relate to legitimacy, but to brute force. So once the influence of IS in Iraq decreases due to a shift to non-sectarian policy, it will become more and more apparent that IS is less an actor seeking justice for the people it claims to fight for, but rather an actor pursuing its own interests.

Osama bin Laden used to justify Jihad in terms of political or religious legitimacy: the Jihad in Afghanistan in the 1980s aimed at defending fellow

Muslims against the unprovoked Soviet invasion; the attack on the US embassy in Mogadishu, as well as on the US military camp in Saudi Arabia, aimed at expelling US troops from the Arabian Peninsula (Kepel 2002: 313-323). It is basically two fatwas which are crucial for today's global Jihad: Bin Laden's "Declaration of Jihad against the Americans Occupying the Land of the Two Holiest Sites" of 1996, and "Jihad Against Jews and Crusaders" in 1998 by Bin Laden, Zawahiri, and others. In those documents, among the presence of US troops in the land of Mecca and Medina, Bin Laden names violence against Muslims in Palestine, Bosnia, Tajikistan, Burma, Kashmir, Assam, Philippine, Fattani, Ugadin, Somalia, Eritrea, or Chechnya as reasons why it is a duty to fight the Americans and its allies. Furthermore, American imperialism is blamed for poverty and social injustice in Muslim countries (Bin Laden 1996; World Islamic Front 1998). The 9/11 terror attacks, the reemerged Jihad hotspot in Afghanistan, as well as the one in Iraq, were justified along similar lines and thereby found sympathy not only among many Muslims, but even among parts of the anti-imperialist left (Taaffe).

IS, however, inherited Zawahiri's very broad and loose concept of *takfir*, which is an Islamic concept of declaring someone's belief heretic and therefore paving the way to declaring someone or a group an enemy in Jihad. As a consequence, this highly arbitrary paradigm of choosing the target opened up the concept of Jihad to a broad variety of goals. Following an order of Zawahiri, Zarqawi changed the name of his al-Qaeda in Mesopotamia to Islamic State of Iraq and declared the creation of an Islamic caliphate the first goal of Jihad in Iraq (Roberts, 2014). Thus, pursuing this profane goal of conquering land for the extension of Islamic State's territory and declaring any opponent in that an enemy in Jihad lacks the broad base of legitimacy Bin Laden's global Jihad sought to establish from the 1990s to at least 2005.

Nevertheless, the Jihad hotspots in Syria and Iraq will continue to attract delusional people from all over the world who are seeking their existential fulfilment in Jihadi adventure. However, without local and international sources of legitimacy, like the first global Jihad hotspot in Afghanistan or the anti-imperialist and pan-Arabic arguments, Syria and Iraq have no potential of becoming sustainable battlegrounds of Jihad. Besides the fact that IS in Syria and in Iraq not only discredited itself as a legitimate actor for the people of Syria and Iraq, it discredits the ideology of Political Islam as a whole: IS's ambitions of power and self-interest strongly add to the disenchantment with Political Islam as an Islamic means to pursue social and political justice.

A transformed role of Political Islam

To sum up, several developments from late 2010 onwards in the MENA region have led to profound reconfigurations of Political Islam. On the one hand, it was the discovery of the effectiveness of social protests in Egypt and Tunisia which shattered the monopoly of Political Islam. On the other hand, IS's display of self-interest and brute force discredited it as a trustworthy representative of Muslim people's social and political demands. All that led to the erosion of the traditional foundations of Political Islam and discredited it as a long-time exclusive and trustworthy means of pursuing political and social justice.

In the short term, Political Islam will still be perceived as being on the rise. But its national and regional foundations have already been eroded. That is why, in the long term, its parties like the Muslim Brotherhood, Hamas, and Tunisia's Ennahda will likely become just one political party among others, rather than the hegemonic threat of everyday politics.

The current Jihad hotspots have been fundamentally fuelled by the golden years of Political Islam from the 1970 until the 2000s in Tunisia, Algeria, Egypt, Palestine, or Syria. However, following the erosion of its national power base, Political Islam will also not be able to be as influential in regional and global affairs as it used to be. Whereas there is still enough money and weapons to maintain its influence by force, and foreign support in fighters and weapons, its role in regional and global affairs will diminish with its original source of power long gone.

Notes

1. Unlike the more or less manifest Islamist and secular factions within the protesting mass in Tunisia and Egypt, it was also various tribal and sectarian factions who opposed former president Saleh in Yemen, either demanding the secession of its Shiite Northwest like the Huthis, or the secession of South Yemen like the Southern Movement ('Who's who in Yemen's opposition?' 2011). In Libya, it was to a large extent a coalition of Eastern Libyan tribes which demanded the ouster of Gadhafi. Thus, whereas the protests in Tunisia and Egypt were predominantly aimed at changing the political nature of its government, various factions within the oppositions in Libya and Yemen had sectarian and regional interests (Fattah 2011).
2. The fact that the military's supreme leader ran for office and was elected by 96.6 percent of the votes already raised first suspicions that the president-elect Sisi will not support the political liberalization of Egypt. Further indications, like the detainment of three Al-Jazeera journalists ('Journalism under fire' 2014), as well as new regulations for civil society organizations (Majeed 2014), also nourish doubts about autocratic tendencies of Egypt's government.

3. The Taliban war against the Soviet Union is considered the first hotspot of global Jihad: Muslims from all around the world were offered the possibility to practice their faith through Jihad. That was, at the same time, the creation of what later became al-Qaeda, literally meaning "base", as in base of Jihad. Many of those Muslims who were trained in the armed Jihad in Afghanistan then deployed to Bosnia to fight the Serbs (Kepel 2002: 217-253, 299-322). And it already was Osama bin Laden and his companion Ayman Az-Zawahiri who orchestrated these activities. Following the US invasion in Afghanistan and the al-Qaeda-led reactivation of this Jihad hotspot, the creation of such hotspots was declared an objective in al-Qaeda strategy papers. The war in Iraq following the US occupation was already intentionally initiated by al-Qaeda affiliate al-Zarqawi (Fisk 2006: 1097-1286). Thus, the situations of political vacuum and turmoil in Libya and Syria were highly welcomed opportunities for al-Qaeda and its global Jihadis (Mortada 2012).

References

al-Din al-Afghani, J. (2003). 'Islamic Union', in Gettlemann, M. and Schaar, S. (ed.) *The Middle East and Islamic World Reader*. New York: Grove Press.

'Algeria: The Revolution that never was', *Al Jazeera*. 17 May 2012. http://www.aljazeera.com/programmes/peopleandpower/2012/05/2012516145457232336.html [3 Sep 2014].

al-Husri, S. (1976). 'Muslim Unity and Arab Unity', in Haim S. (ed.) *Arab Nationalism: An Anthology*. California: University of California Press.

'Al-Zarqawi declares war on Iraqi Shia'. *Al Jazeera* (14 September 2005). http://www.aljazeera.com/archive/2005/09/200849143727698709.html [3 Sep 2014].

Bin Laden, O. (1996). 'Declaration of Jihad Against the Americans Occupying the Land of the Two Holiest Sites'.

Dawisa, A. (2005). *Arab Nationalism in the Twentieth Century: From Triumph to Despair*. Princeton, NJ: Princeton University Press.

Dergham, R. (2012). 'Fears of the Arab Spring Becoming an "Islamist Spring"'. *The World Post*. 20 January 2012. http://www.huffingtonpost.com/raghida-dergham/fears-of-the-arab-spring-_b_1219834.html [25 Aug 2014].

Fattah, K. (2011). 'Tribes and Tribalism in the Arab Spring', *CEMMIS: Center for Mediterranean, Middle East and Islamic Studies*. 26 October 2011. [3 Sep 2014].

Fisk, R. (2006). *The Great War for Civilisation: The Conquest of the Middle East*. London et al.: Harper Perennial.

Hourani, A. (2005): *A History of the Arab Peoples*. London: Faber and Faber.

'Journalism under Fire: Free AJStaff'. *Al Jazeera*. http://www.aljazeera.com/indepth/spotlight/freeajstaff/ [3 Sep 2014].

Kepel, G. (2003). *Jihad: The Trial of Political Islam*. Londres: Belknap Press.

Majeed, J. (2014). 'Growing Restrictions on Egyptian Civil Society as Parliamentary Elections Loom Closer'. *Human Rights First*. 30 July 2014. http://www.humanrightsfirst.org/blog/growing-restrictions-egyptian-civil-society-parliamentary-elections-loom-closer [3 Sep 2014].

Maudūdī, A. (1955). *Islamic Law and Constitution*. Karachi: Jamaat-e-Islami Publications.

Mortada, R. (2012). 'Bilad al-Sham: Jihad's Newest Hot Spot'. *Al-Akhbar*. 6 August 2012. http://english.al-akhbar.com/node/10806 [4 Sep 2014].

Mouloudj, M. (2014). 'Né dans le sillage de l'opposition à un 4e mandat pour Bouteflika: Où est passé le mouvement Barakat ?'. *Liberté Algerie*. 27 July 2014. http:/www.liberte-algerie.com/dossiers/o-est-passe-le-mouvement-barakat-ne-dans-le-sillage-de-l-opposition-a-un-4e-mandat-pour-bouteflika-225735 [4 Sep 2014].

Quṭb, S. (2007). Milestones, Chicago, IL: Kazi Publications.

Roberts, N. (2014). 'The (non) Islamic State: Abu Bakr al-Baghdadi and the Challenge of Islamic Illiteracy'.*The Middle East Monitor*. 31 July 2014. https://www.middleeastmonitor.com/articles/middle-east/13144-the-non-islamic-state-abu-bakr-al-baghdadi-and-the-challenge-of-islamic-illiteracy [4 Sep 2014].

Spencer R. (2012). 'Middle East review of 2012: the Arab Winter'. *The Telegraph*. 31 December 2012. http://www.telegraph.co.uk/news/worldnews/middleeast/9753123/Middle-East-review-of-2012-the-Arab-Winter.html [25 Aug 2014].

Spencer, R. (2014). *Arab Winter Comes to America: The Truth About the War We're In.* Washington, D.C.: Regnery Publishing.

Taaffe, P. 'Afghanistan, Islam and the Revolutionary Left'. *socialistworld.net.* http://www.socialistworld.net/pubs/afghanistan/afghanchp5.html [4 Sep 2014].

Weber, M. (1978). *Economy and Society: An Outline of Interpretative Sociology. Volume One.* Berkeley et al.: University of California Press.

'Who's who in Yemen's opposition?' *Al Jazeera* (28 February 2011). http://www.aljazeera.com/indepth/spotlight/yemen/2011/02/2011228141453986337.html [3 Sep 2014].

'Jihad Against Jews and Crusaders'. *World Islamic Front.* 23 February 1998.

2

Imamate and Caliphate: Islamic Governance Theory in Moroccan Islamist Discourse

JUAN A. MACÍAS-AMORETTI
UNIVERSITY OF GRANADA, SPAIN

Ideological and political background of Moroccan Islamism

Political Islam is a very wide ideological concept that includes diverse political movements and trends (Khan, 2014). A common element to all of them is the use of the 'Islamic reference' (*al-marji'iyya al-islâmiyya*) as the foundation of their political practice. Establishing the 'Islamic state' (*tatbîq al-dawla al-islâmiyya*) is the main goal of their political action, and this very concept sets Islamist political action within the framework of political modernity. Yet, while Islamist movements try to track their political legitimacy to the 'prophetic' action, they have to face many ideological challenges to adapt Islamic concepts and theories from 'classical' jurisprudence to modern political competition. This is the case of Moroccan political Islam, including major actors as the Justice and Development Party (PJD)[1] and the Community of Justice and Spirituality (CJS)[2]. Both of them do develop an Islamic theory on governance in their discourse, trying to adapt classical concepts as 'imamate' (*imâma*) or 'caliphate' (*khilâfa*) to their own ideological conception of power and to their specific situation in political competition.

To start with, there are many aspects dealing with political Islam as a political actor in Morocco. Most of the organisations belonging to what is called the 'Islamic movement' (*al-haraka al-islâmiyya*) in Morocco do share a historical background, from its first emergence in the early 70s when the first Islamic political organisations came up as an ideological response to the declining leftist secular opposition to the 'Alawi Monarchy regime. They also share an epistemological combination of *ikhwâni* –influenced by the political action of the Muslim Brotherhood – and *da'wi* – influenced by charitable religious associations – elements. Among these, the two most influential organisations of Moroccan political Islam, in quantitative and qualitative terms, are the Community of Justice and Spirituality (*Jamâ'at al-'Adl wa-l-Ihsân* [CJS]), and the Unicity and Reform Movement (*Harakat al-Tawhîdwa-l-Islâh* [MUR])[3] – politically linked with the Justice and Development Party (*Hizb al-'Adâlawa-l-Tanmiyya* [PJD]) from the latter 90s. The CJS is an outsider, but visible, movement located outside the boundaries of the regime in terms of non-violent political resistance, while the PJD is a main institutional political actor located in the parliamentary opposition up to 2011 when it reached the government in coalition with other political parties.

Hence, Political Islam today is the expression of an ideological and political alternative in Morocco that underlines Islamic morality as a core element. Islamist ideologues, such as Abdelilah Ben Kiran (b. 1954), the Secretary General of the PJD and Moroccan Prime Minister from 2011, or Abdessalam Yassine (1928-2012), the charismatic founder and leader of the CJS, claim to derive the foundation of their Islamic political action from the Islamic moral reference. That said, they chose almost opposite ways of dealing with political power in the country. In this sense, the moral element in their political discourse does represent an attempt to draw a whole new contemporary 'Islamic narrative' (as political Islam is not a 'traditionalist' movement) and, therefore, to present the historical dynamic of political Islam as a movement that is essentially moral and 'prophetic', as it foresees a specific kind of Islamic utopia, and translating it in the discourse in terms of real democracy and social justice.

This alleged religious (moral) legitimacy is a central reference in the use of ideology (Macías-Amoretti, 2014) as an almost exclusive resource in competing for power with the primary and secondary elites (Izquierdo Brichs, 2012). Thus, the Islamist alternative in Morocco is based on a political and social ideology that is founded on a religious discourse of political change (democracy) and social reform (justice), filled with concepts derived from the juridical tradition of classical Islam, but which are *politicised* in their origin (production of discourse-input) and *re-politicised* in the discourse (reproduction of discourse-output), and based pragmatically on the conditions of competition for power in Morocco and the position of each of the Islamist actors in this setting. The main specific factor here is linked with the specificity of the religious and political context of contemporary Morocco. In this sense, the non-negligible role of the 'Alawi Monarchy in the country must be mentioned. Indeed, its sovereigns possess a symbolic capital that irrefutably legitimizes their position as political and religious leaders, and decisively situates power relations within the framework of the state itself.

According to current Moroccan Constitution (reformed in 2011) the King of Morocco –Muhammad VI from 1999 – holds the title of 'amîr al-mu'minîn' (Commander of the Faithful). This is something that is not a mere symbol. It implies the religious legitimacy of his power as the 'emirate', one of the most important titles historically held by the Sunni Caliphs, referring originally to their highest military powers (Belal, 2012). The King of Morocco is not merely the head of the Moroccan state, a modern and secular Muslim state-nation, but is also the highest religious authority and the personification of the Islamic community leadership in the country and even outside it, as the Moroccan 'imârat al-mu'minîn' is recognized by other Islamic authorities in Western Africa and among the Moroccan diaspora. In political terms, it is not possible to refuse the legal authority of the 'Alawi Monarchy from an 'Islamic' point of view, as their political power is inseparable from their religious legitimacy (Darif, 2010). This status makes the Islamic political action of political Islam in Morocco far more ideological than in other Muslim contexts. The use of juridical and political Islamic concepts as the 'imamate' (*imâma*) and the 'caliphate' (*khilâfa*) by main Moroccan Islamist actors PJD and CJS in their discourse are thus directly linked to the monarchical 'imârat al-mu'minîn' in terms of acceptance-reform or refusing-resistance. In that sense, it is therefore linked to a concrete model of 'Islamic government' in ideological terms.

'Imamate', political leadership, and power in the PJD's discourse

The nature of the PJD's political discourse is linked with its participative approach (Wegner, 2011). Since its initial debates, the PJD accepted the religious and political legitimacy of the 'imârat al-mu'minîn', and from this very clear stance it has attempted to present its political model of governance. The ideological foundations of such model are based on the full compatibility and suitability of the moral and legal principles of the sharia – guaranteed by the 'imârat al-mu'minîn' – with democratic principles and the political role of consensus reforming the political system from within. In this way, the aim of the PJD and the MUR is to establish an Islamic state in moral and legal terms, by applying democratic methods, namely free-competition elections. In the MUR's discourse, the call to da'wa, preach to Islamic values, lies at the heart of a democratic theory which is understood as a set of political techniques. The democratic principles to which the party's discourse subscribes are: popular sovereignty (*al-siyâda li-l-sha'b*), division of powers (*fasl al-sulat al-thalâtha*), and the guarantee of rights and freedoms (*damân al-huqûqwa-l-hurriyyât*). However, its theoretical development shows certain particular characteristics that link these democratic principles with the principles of Islamic theory on governance based on the 'imamate', in which the only real sovereignty and the highest legislative power belong to God alone. This well-structured democratic discourse, however, is set within the power struggle of a secondary elite that aspires to become a primary one. Thus, the party attempts to adapt its ideological discourse to the expectations of society on one hand, and on the other, to exceed the resources of the competing elites by trying to turn itself into a political actor that is singularised by its Islamic discourse and practice in moral terms. The PJD's discourse is therefore adapted to the circumstances of political competition, so it is sometimes populist, but it always acknowledges the Islamic legitimacy of the monarchy at the top.

The concept of the 'imamate' (*imâma*) is used by the PJD as a synonym of 'straightaway governance' in moral terms (*al-hukm al-râshid*). As such, it is not definitely a unipersonal institution as it used to be understood in classical Sunni Islamic thought – linked to the spiritual attributions and the 'supreme leadership' of the Caliph as successor to the Prophet Muhammad. Rather, it is to be understood as a general framework of good governance, a kind of prophetic moral guideline (el-Outhmani, 2010). According to the party's conceptual reference, political activity in 21st century Morocco is a matter of 'imamate', as it is a religious affair and must be implemented in the name of Islam. The PJD states that Islamic political governance should be useful to the Muslim community and always endorsed by Islamic principles. The organic political action can be adapted to the changing circumstances, taking different shapes as a movement, political party, or juridical disposition implemented from the government, in the case of the PJD, keeping in mind that the 'imamate' is understood as the 'spiritual direction and organization' of a 'Civil State' (*dawla madaniyya*). This state – which is already an Islamic state (*dawla islâmiyya*) – fully complements the 'imamate' to the 'imârat al-mu'minîn' in political and religious terms, as they both are part of the Islamic leadership that guarantees the implementation of Islam and its moral values and juridical rules in Moroccan society.

As the PJD's official discourse states, reform (*islâh*) and renewal (*tajdîd*) are two fundamental elements in the political ideology and discourse of the party. This discourse always takes Islam as its main reference point, and any political action is endorsed by the authority of Islam (*al-marji'iyya al-islâmiyya*). This authority emphatically declares Morocco to be essentially a Muslim country. It also proposes to politically fight against 'deviations' (*inhirâf*), these mainly being a relaxation in morals and habits and the negative influence of poorly-focused Western modernity (PJD, 2002). Therefore, the party's discourse views moralising (*al-takhlîq*) as the necessary starting point for political action to end corruption in public administration. Thus, their discourse is pragmatic and attempts to create a mobilising ideology that ensures the support of very diverse sectors of Moroccan population, especially around the idea of fighting against corruption. In practical terms, the PJD has clearly made more efforts in this area than the other institutional actors, and this has strengthened its support by society and, in short, smoothed the way of the party to power in 2011. Generally speaking, the PJD's political discourse is highly pragmatic, founded on a conception of religion as a basic element of its ideology that includes political praxis for the purpose of improving the living standards of believers; or rather, political activity conceived as 'good and useful action' ('*amal sâlih mufîd*). Through the discursive development of these principles, the PJD considers that there is no incompatibility between Islam and democracy, a view that is basically an attempt to justify the party's participation in the Moroccan political system as a competing elite and, therefore, as an essential actor and an intrinsic part of the actual system (insider), and, at the same time, legitimising the system's validity from an Islamic standpoint. In this context, the PJD has been notable in a positive sense for encouraging high levels of internal democracy in its national congresses. Likewise, the party recognises Morocco's religious plurality, considering Moroccan Jews to be citizens with full rights, though Islam is considered to be the nation's religious, identity, and cultural benchmark. In the field of external relations, the PJD's discourse stresses the need to strengthen diplomatic, economic, and commercial ties with the rest of the Arab and Islamic world as a priority. In practice, the party has strengthened its ties with the main world powers, guaranteeing stability and cooperation in maintaining the market economy and the application of neoliberal formulas.

Spiritual 'caliphate' and political government in the CJS's discourse

The political theory of the CJS was devised to frame the historical and methodological progress of the definitive transition from 'the tyrannical, oppressive government' (*al-hukm al-jabrî*) – or rather, the Moroccan regime symbolised by the 'Alawi Monarchs – to the Islamic Caliphate (*al-khilâfa al-islâmiyya*) made up of the progressive union of different national Islamic states (emirates) headed by their own emirs. The claim for a 'caliphate' is directly launched against the temporal powers of the Moroccan king as 'amîr al-mu'minîn', and it seeks a higher moral legitimacy holding a deep spiritual and even mystical meaning. In his famous work The Prophetic Path (*al-Minhâj al-nabawî*), Abdessalam Yassine did point out that the majority of Muslim believers, regardless of nationality, must uphold the Islamic system (Yassine, 2001). He defended the re-unification of the whole Muslim world in a single political structure that guarantees the 'government of Islam' led by the principles contained in the Quran and the Sunna. According to Yassine, these principles could be adapted to the changing social, political, and economic circumstances of the time by implementing a deep 'reform' (*islâh*) and a 'renewal' (*tajdîd*) in moral terms, keeping faith and spirituality on top. The above-mentioned political structure is based on the 'government of the *shûrà*' (*hukm al-shûrà*) or *shûrà-cracy*. In practical terms, it would be a kind of pyramidal and highly hierarchical structure, with the figure of the 'emir' on top, as he should be responsible for any decision and action made by the state in any possible field. On the other hand, the 'emir' must accept internal criticism and reach consensus following the Quranic commandment of 'mutual consultation' (*shûrà*), so he must be supported and advised by a 'Consultation Council' (*majlis al-shûrà*). Yet the 'emir' is a political figure, according to his attributions. He must be legitimated by the act of allegiance (*bay'a*) as a religious leader symbolically considered the successor to the prophet Muhammad. To Yassine, the recourse to the bay'a guarantees also the free election of the leader, and implicitly rejects the hereditary model represented by the Moroccan monarchy and by the historical caliphate from the early Umayyad period (late 7th c. A.D.). As a successor to the Prophet, the 'emir' is literally a 'Caliph' in spiritual terms, and it is from this spiritual perspective that the CJS understands this figure, far away from the historical and political restoration vindications of other Islamist movements. From a 'regional' perspective, the political structures of each Muslim country would be transformed peacefully by the ideological work and the education, according to the CJS's discourse, into regional Islamic states headed by their respective 'emirs' and ruled by the '*shûrà-cracy*'. Those states would be then unified within the structure of a single caliphate with moral and spiritual attributions. The believers must support the progressive advance of these emirates and caliphate structures in any case, but Islamic organisations such as the CJS are seen as being at the vanguard of the movement by their active educative work and their ideological consciousness, thus seemingly in a lineal structure of power. This progressive movement of liberation and unification would always be implemented by peaceful means in different stages, the first and most important one them being the substitution of the 'despotic government' (*al-hukm al-mustabidd*) by the 'government of the *shûrà* (*hukm al-shûrà*). This stage would be followed by the general call to the 'real' Islamic message in moral and spiritual terms, and the implementation of the Islamic education, and finally by the economic and political 'liberation' of the Islamic Umma. Bearing in mind the moral parameter, the 'caliphate' is linked here to the improvement of the social and economic conditions of the Muslim people by liberating them from the dependence of external financial resources and internal corruption, so implementing a 'real Islamic economy' and bringing back national economic resources to Muslim hands. To the CJS, when the economy is adapted to the moral principles contained in the Quran and the Sunna, mainly to the Islamic values of 'justice' (*'adl*) and 'solidarity with the left out people' (*insâf*), only then is a real Islamic government possible. These are thus the moral foundations of the Islamic caliphate defended by the association. This Islamic discourse is addressed directly in the name of Islam to the Moroccan monarchy, whose kings are delegitimised as 'emirs' and represent to the CJS the negative values of the 'other' in moral terms (tyranny, despotism, hypocrisy).

In the CJS discourse, the democratic parameters are compared as a set of negative moral values with the positive ideal of the Islamic *'shûrà-cracy'*. Democracy is associated with secularism, and thus it is viewed as a 'Western' cultural product that is morally inferior and not extrapolated to the Islamic political and cultural tradition. The alternative to democracy is the *shûrà*, with the sharia as its legal foundation. Clearly, the structure of this political and social system, and the way it would be introduced, is not sufficiently developed in the CJS discourse, in which it represents an ideal for mobilising the people, but without any detailed particulars. In spite of this discourse on the *shûrà*, the structure of the CJS is organised into a singular pyramidal power system, where absolute political leadership is indisputably exerted by the Secretary General along with the 'Political Circle' (*al-dâ'ira al-siyâsiyya*), and legitimated by an unshakeable spiritual link to the Guide-General. The relationship between the CJS and the so-called 'official Islam' is one of negation. The CJS does not recognise the institution of the *imârat al-mu'minîn* as the attributed right of the 'Alawi monarchy, instead believing that this attribution of caliphal powers is unlawful. This stance, just like all the movement's discourse in general, is set within a power struggle in which the resource of ideology – based on the legitimacy of a specific interpretation of Islam in a political sense – plays a central role. Thus the CJS's discourse once again stresses the Islamic moral element as a power resource.

Conclusions

The wide diversity of ideological options in Moroccan Political Islam is manifested in a broad Islamist discourse that shares a series of fundamental elements that link the concepts of *imâma* and *khilâfa*, from the moral and legal standpoint of Islamic reform (*islâh*), to that of *imârat al-mu'minînin* terms of acceptance/reformism or refuse/resistance. However, the discourse of Islamist parties and movements as the PJD or the CJS differs in terms of the more pragmatic or strategic elements they use, as it must be borne in mind that the ideological element is the essential power resource for them, and it is by using this resource that each of them attempts to turn itself into a main political actor and into a moral point of reference within the framework of political competition for power in Morocco. The main vector of their discourse and the ideology that backs it up (and which essentially frames Islamist political practice) is the use of Islamic moral references linking the role of Islamic governance to the governed, and the role of the 'Islamic state' to the citizens-believers, in the vanguard of which (either in resistance, opposition, or reformism) each of the actors in Moroccan political Islam claim to be situated.

Notes

1. Justice and Development Party (http://www.pjd.ma)
2. Community of Justice and Spirituality (http://www.aljamaa.net)
3. Unicity and Reform Movement (http://www.alislah.ma)

References

Belal, Y. Le cheikh et le caliphe. *Sociologie religieuse de l'islam politique au Maroc*. Casablanca: Tarik éditions. (2012).

Darif, M. *Monarchie marocaine et acteurs religieux*. Casablanca: Afrique orient. (2010).

el-Outhmani, S.E. *Al-Dîn wa-l-siyâsâ. Tamayyîz lâ fasl*. Casablanca/Beirut: al-Markaz al-Thaqâfî l-'Arabî. (2009).

Izquierdo Brichs, F. (ed.) *Political Regimes in the Arab World: Society and the Exercise of Power*. London: Routledge. (2012).

Khan, M. 'What is political Islam?' *E-International Relations*. (2014). Published electronically http://www.e-ir.info/2014/03/10/what-is-political-islam/

Macías-Amoretti, J.A. 'Political Islam: discourse, ideology and power'. *E-International Relations*. (2014). Published electronically http://www.e-ir.info/2014/03/03/political-islam-discourse-ideology-and-power/.

PJD. *Farîq al-'Adâlawa-l-Tanmiyyabi Majlis al-Nuwâb: hasîlat al-sanawât al-khamsiltizāmwa 'atâ', 1997-2002*. Rabat: PJD. (2002).

Wegner, E. *Islamist Opposition in Authoritarian Regimes. The Party of Justice and Development in Morocco*. Syracuse: Syracuse University Press. (2011).

Yassine, A. *Al-Minhâj al-nabawî: tarbiyyawa-tanzîmwa-zahf*, 4th ed., Casablanca, Dâr al-Afâq. (2001).

3

Legal Pluralism and Sharia: Implementing Islamic Law in States and Societies

ADEL ELSAYED SPARR
UNIVERSITY OF UPPSALA, SWEDEN

Introduction

Between multiculturalism and islamophobia, allowing sharia to govern certain aspects of Muslim lives has emerged as a frequently debated issue in several Western countries, such as the UK[1], the USA (Macfarlane, 2012), Australia, France[2], Germany[3], Canada[4], and so on. This debate is no less vivid in predominantly Muslim countries. For instance, Article 2 of the Egyptian constitution makes the principles of sharia *the* primary source of legislation. This specific article has remained since 1980, before which the principles of sharia were *a* primary source of legislation. Furthermore, note that the principles of sharia are being referenced – not sharia as such – but what this ambiguous formulation means in practice is unclear (Brown, 2002:181). Moreover, in Lebanon, each large denomination has its own jurisdiction in matters of family law, which is reflected in the existence of Shia, Sunni, Christian, Jewish, and secular civil courts – and yet, the highest court of appeal is the national and secular Court of Cassation (Mallat, 1997:31). The questions range from what sharia is, which Islamic jurisprudential tradition should be permitted, to what extent sharia may govern the lives of Muslims, and what legal areas should be influenced by sharia. In times when violent and radical fundamentalist groups such as Boko Haram, ISIL, or al-Shabaab, for instance, use their (mis)interpretation of sharia to legitimise their abominable actions – often as means to an end, i.e. the establishment of an Islamic state or caliphate – it becomes imperative to discuss and clarify what sharia actually is.

So what role does sharia play in today's societies? What role can it play? What role should it have? And what potential does it have? All these questions have become ever so pertinent in a globalised world, where the increasing mobility of people has led to increased cultural diversity that challenges national identities and thus erodes the nation-state. From a socio-legal perspective, multiculturalism creates legislative challenges. In abstract, a law corresponds to a social norm and contains a moral distinction between right and wrong. However, having a single body of national law contradicts the features of a multicultural society, in which different norms compete. The solution has been legal pluralism, which Woodman defines as the "condition in which a population observes more than one body of law" (1999:3). Consequently, the most important overarching question is what the implications of legal pluralism are.

This article will address this question in order to shed light on the present status of sharia in an international system of nation-states and increasingly diverse societies, ethnically, culturally, and religiously. I will argue that although sharia has the potential to overcome certain challenges to govern a multicultural society, insofar as it is considered by some to be the only legitimate source of legislation for Muslims, gradual introduction of legal pluralism in a nation-state will incrementally delegitimise the state. Instead, I propose a reinterpretation of sharia, which will constitute the basis for political organisation. If Muslims want sharia norms to govern, they must get representation in the legislature by ways of an equal citizenship – which has to be the common denominator in any nation-state – and democratic deliberation. Subsequently, this endeavour requires an understanding and definition of what sharia is, which the article initially provides. It then moves on to ask why people obey the law, as the answer to that constitutes the basis for realising why legal pluralism is not compatible with the notion of a legitimate nation-state. The article ends with a suggestion about how to deal with the call for legal pluralism – in this case, an urge to permit sharia as a legal code alongside national law – which grows stronger when societies become more multicultural.

The path to the waterhole

There is an important distinction to be made between sharia and Islamic law (Brown, 1997:363). While sharia literally means the path to the waterhole and constitutes the totality of the normative system for Muslims, Islamic law is the legal system inspired by those principles. According to an-Na'im[6], sharia is a "human endeavour to understand the divine", and as such, it can never per se be divine. Thus, there is no such thing as sharia *law*; only law inspired by sharia, i.e. Islamic law, which per definition is man-made. Consequently, Islamic law is suppositional and not divine, since it is fundamentally the product of what Muslim scholars and jurists suppose is God's idea of right and wrong. When both Muslims and critics of sharia conflate Islamic norms of right and wrong with Islamic law, jurisprudence, and punishments, the question of introducing sharia is asked in the wrong way. Muslims in general consider legitimate legal sovereignty to belong to the divine sharia, as opposed to the people. Thus, any institution that can attach itself to sharia and claim its authority will command this for Muslims' legitimate legal sovereignty as well. If such institutions, for instance al-Azhar in Cairo or the Guardian Council in Iran, are co-opted in a political regime, they enable political actors to obtain legitimacy for their decisions (Abou El Fadl, 2012:55). Islam can be used for such purposes as well. This essentially builds on the inaccurate notion that sharia is divine, and that Islamic law is not suppositional. Moreover, because of this, Islamic law is manipulated to conform to certain political interests of subduction. The modernisation of Islamic jurisprudence and law is therefore a matter of political will more than anything else, and so is its implementation in a state. As soon as Islamic law is enacted by the state, it ceases to be the will of God – if it ever were – and becomes the political will of the state (An-Na'im, 2013).

Is it hypothetically possible for sharia to adjust to a modern society? Consider the examples of Christianity and Judaism. The Old Testament is full of provisions that are seriously abhorrent to the most moderate human rights advocate. Still, very few Christians or Jews would propose that rebellious children should be stoned to death (Book of Deuteronomy[7,] 21:18-21), or that if a man commits adultery with another man's wife, both shall be put to death (Book of Leviticus[8], 20:10). Disobeying a parent – unless the parent is abusive – or having an affair are examples of immoral actions, and the moral principle is still that both acts are wrong, but the social norm regarding their punishment has radically changed. Similarly, the normative system of sharia stipulates that having extramarital sexual intercourse, which would be considered zina, is morally wrong. However, the punishment for adultery is one hundred lashes, according to the Quran (24:29), and stoning to death, according to the hadith of Sahih Muslim (17:419410). Such punishments are hardly compatible with modern societies, but if Christianity and Judaism could modernise from this status, so can Islam.

The question of why Islamic jurisprudence has not modernised is debatable – even the very premise that it has not, cannot be taken for granted. Arguably, however, it has yet to modernise. In the 9th century, the legal schools formed and taqlid was subsequently introduced. This closed the door to *ijtihad*, and no new interpretations of the legal sources were made. Indeed, an-Na'im do acknowledge that although there were some developments and adaptation through *fiqh* since *taqlid* was introduced, they took place within the methodology and structure of sharia that were already established before *taqlid*, which thus remained ever since (2005:42). This historical account is to be understood through another historical development, i.e. the conflict between *ahl al-ra`y* and ahl *al-hadith*, which preceded *taqlid*. The former were those who argued that law should be understood through logic and reasoning – proponents of *ijtihad* – as opposed to the latter, who advocated an exclusive adherence to the Quran and *hadith* regarding legal thought (Shalakany, 2013:12). This conflict was resolved by the institutionalisation of *fiqh*, but fundamentally meant that *ahl al-hadit*h became the reigning paradigm in Islamic legal thought.

What, then, would be necessary to modernise Islamic law and punishments, while retaining the moral principles of sharia that, for instance, adultery is wrong? In an open letter[11] to the leader of ISIL, Abu Bakr al-Baghdadi, 126 very prominent Sunni scholars – for instance the Grand Mufti of Egypt, professors from al-Azhar, and several Sheikhs from the Fatwa Council of Egypt – conclude that virtually every act committed by ISIL is forbidden in Islam. Furthermore, they establish that it is necessary for legal scholars to consider the "reality of contemporary times when deriving legal rulings", a practice which is called *fiqh al-wāqi'*, literally meaning the jurisprudence of reality. This opens up for a consideration of the modern global context in Islamic legal reasoning. Above all, it provides an authoritative hint that *ijtihad* should be practiced. Moreover, reintroducing the legal principles of *istihsan* and *istislah* would also make a good start to modernise sharia, because they rely on the social context and reality as opposed to literal interpretation of the legal sources. As is clear, there are jurisprudential tools available within Islam that can update and modernise fiqh, and it is against this background that the question of permitting sharia must be understood.

Forced to be free

Essentially, laws always reflect activities that a given community at a given time disapproves of and perceives as illegitimate. Moreover, political legitimacy is derived from legitimate laws, and the latter emerges through a conscientious behaviour of obedience (cf. Higgins, 2004:1-47). This is important, because it tells us why the political legitimacy of a nation-state is threatened if its laws are illegitimate. A nation-state needs to be founded and maintained by a conscientious behaviour of obedience. But what does such a behaviour emerge from? Why do people obey the law? And what is it that makes laws legitimate? These are no simple or small questions, and probably require a more thorough and exhaustive analysis to answer than what can be offered here. Thus, the outline below will have to suffice as a primer to the political and legal theory of legitimate laws.

Some argue that in a procedural democracy, the legitimacy of laws depends on whether the legislative process is accepted by the subjects of those laws or not (Allard-Tremblay, 2013:381). However, there is no prima facie obligation to obey the law; as Raz points out, "the fact that a legal system is just is not a reason to obey it" (1979:245). The problem can be understood through the relationship between legality and legitimacy, where the former does not imply the latter. The laws of the European Union, for instance, have legality but lack legitimacy (Kratochwil, 2006:303). Law is legitimate only if its claims to obedience get assent amongst its subjects independent of content (Higgins, 2004:6). The lack of such assent is exactly why Muslims – or other denominations in today's nation-states – demand sharia and pledge obedience to it, as opposed to national state law. Religious belief is obviously the explicated reason to why Muslims demand sharia, but if Islamic jurisprudence can modernise as described above, then sharia could arguably conform to national laws on a political level.

Subsequently, the political theory that underscores the nation-state is social contract theory of some sorts. The political theory of Rousseau is relevant in this regard, because the constituent principle in Rousseau's legitimate state is the law, which justifies the state's existence spiritually by making the social contract's associates politically free (Putterman, 2010). The assumption is that two contradicting interests politically drive people: freedom and security. The state is the solution meant to accommodate these interests, but the cardinal problem for any associational state is this accommodation. Rousseau argued that "the people, being subjected to the laws, should be the authors of them; it concerns only the associates to determine the conditions of association" (1762:179, II:VI:10). The social contract generates to general will, which forces people to obey the law. This means they obey themselves, but they do not obey a ruler; they obey the law, and only the law that they themselves have decreed (Cohen, 2010:136). In this context, Rousseau's maxim "forced to be free" means nothing less than that obeying the law which oneself has prescribed is freedom and security at the same time (Rousseau, 1762:167, I:VIII:§3). If an individual thinks s/he has good, conscientious reasons *not* to obey the law, this corresponds to the will of each, as opposed to the general will. Therefore, s/he shall be forced to be free. Arguably, conscientious obedience in a polity is a behaviour that occurs when existing social norms harmonise with the law of a given polity. Accordingly, law becomes legitimate when it reflects the social norms of a polity. Put differently, when the general will – which is the expression of the normative system of a society – dictates the law, it gets assent from the people independent of content and procedure; there is thus a legitimate and moral obligation to obey the law (Higgins, 2004:3-5).

However, this presupposes that the nation-state is a homogenous polity in terms of social norms, which obviously is not the case. The problem is that Muslims do not feel that the general will dictates on their behalf. The question is more pragmatic than theoretical: how do we make Muslims feel included in the general will? This is a political issue of the social contract.

Legal pluralism – legitimate law, legitimate nation-state, or both?

Before the nation-state emerged as the dominant form of organising power, law was "invariably of sub-state provenance" and reflected the cultural and religious diversity that had always existed in societies (Jackson, 2006:171). The nation-state obscured this diversity by exacerbating a national identity that became unified in a more homogenous culture and often religion, thus suppressing the social diversity. Jackson (2006) argues, furthermore, that law does not have to originate from the nation-state, and that legal pluralism thus can reconcile a diverse society. However, law does not originate from the state; it emerges from the social norms in a given society, and the state acts as a vehicle to express those norms in the form of laws. When different norms compete in a society, can legal systems that correspond to those norms coexist while retaining the political legitimacy of the nation-state? The choice seems to stand between a legitimate nation-state with one body of national law and a homogenous society, or a different form of organising power with multiple bodies of law that correspond to its consenting community. Legal pluralists, on the other hand, argue that there can be a legitimate nation-state and multiple bodies of law that reflect a heterogeneous society.

Legitimate laws stem from the general will of the people. If the people are divided by having multiple general wills, the people will perceive different laws as legitimate – as is the case in plural societies. A nation-state can only have one general will and one legal system for it to be legitimate. A nation-state with multiple general wills is not a state; it is a contradiction. That the same law will apply to each member of society equally is, moreover, an important prerequisite for the rule of law to function properly. Obedience to more than one legal system is to put oneself above the law, because the arbitrary nature of such an act indicates that the law cannot claim authority.

Legal pluralism is, however, an empirical reality. Subsequently, there are empirical problems with legal pluralism. For instance, in crossover situations where the parties in a dispute do not share allegiance to the same legal system, it becomes inherently difficult to decide which legal system is going to arbitrate the dispute (Tamanaha, 2012:40). Furthermore, Twining asserts that the legal pluralism is "not much concerned with normative questions about legitimacy, authority, justification [and] obligatoriness" (2012:121). This can cause political actors to engage in a game of identity politics, and exacerbate identities, which leads to an increasing sense of otherness and alienation (Barzilai, 2008:404-407), and therefore encourage contentious behaviour (Pruitt and Kim, 2004:25-35, 116-118). Moreover, legal pluralism is not inclusive per definition. States can use legal pluralism to promote political control over minorities, which has been the case in the Middle East and elsewhere (Barzilai, 2008:409-416). Specifically for Islam, the empirical reality is that there is not a unified idea of what sharia is. If sharia were implemented, it would be unclear which of the many traditions to implement.

Dealing with the call for legal pluralism

If the solution to plural societies in a nation-state is not a plural jurisdiction, what is the alternative? Legal pluralism is, after all, an empirical reality, and so are social diversity and multiculturalism in the nation-states of today. There are two ways to go, both of which aim to achieve a legitimate form of organising power and legitimate laws. Either we keep the nation-state and try to construct a reality in which a multicultural society can nevertheless perceive itself as *one* society, or we abandon the nation-state as the dominant way of organising power and embrace social diversity under another form of statehood and citizenship. The latter seems much less realistic than the former. Even if the nation-state seems to be fading away in a post-national era, we can probably hold on to it a little longer – and realistically, we probably must. How, then, can we deal with the paradox of permitting sharia alongside national state law, but still retaining legitimate laws in a sovereign nation-state? The answer to how to deal with the call to permit sharia to govern the lives of Muslims has to do with political representation and (re) interpretation of sharia. Pragmatically this means that sharia needs to be accommodated, not permitted.

As argued above, because law serves a political purpose and is always the product of human understanding, knowledge, and reasoning, permitting and implementing the norms of sharia in the form of law is, accordingly, a matter of political deliberation. In fact, an-Na'im argues "that the idea of an Islamic state to enforce sharia as positive state law is incoherent because once principles of sharia are enacted as positive law of a state, they cease to be the religious law of Islam and become the political will of that state" (2013:11f). Instead of demanding sharia, Muslims have the option to organize politically – which is political and not religious – in accordance with this understanding of sharia The legal reforms Muslims would ask for would reflect the normative system of sharia, which is not very different from the human rights-based normative values of a modern nation-state (Sarwar, 2012:247ff). Thus, permitting legal principles in accordance with sharia should instead be understood as a matter of political compromise in a democratically elected legislature.

Indeed, the medieval forms of punishment must not be asked for. This is why modernisation of *fiqh* is needed – and possible. Once the Islamic jurisprudence is modernised and accepted by Muslims and their fellow citizens, a deliberative political dialogue between equal citizens can take place without exclusion, alienation, or islamophobia. In such a reality, a shared citizenship becomes the common denominator and primary identity marker, as opposed to religion, culture, or ethnicity. Essentially, this is what a democratic nation-state is about, and it is arguably what Rousseau would have wanted his associational state to be like. In such a state, there is no need for unanimity in the political decision-making process and legislation. If the interests of Muslims are represented in a democratically elected legislature – which requires an equal citizenship – religion and sharia will not matter; only the general will of which every citizen is part will matter. Sharia as a set of moral values will, *ipso facto*, be implemented and permitted if political representation based on citizenship is strengthened. This would result in a general assent for the laws of a nation-state, which is also shared by Muslims, and the call to permit sharia law is rendered irrelevant. Obviously, this is an idealized scenario, but every political system will be imperfect, and there are strong arguments that the real issue is about representation, citizenship, and political participation – especially if sharia is understood as proposed in this article.

Conclusion

This article has tried to make the question of whether or not to permit sharia to govern Muslims in certain aspects of their lives a non-question. It has analysed the jurisprudential history of sharia in order to establish why it has not modernized and what needs to be done for it to do so. Moreover, it has argued that because sharia is human and not divine, it always serves a political purpose. To this extent, the implementation of sharia in nation-states alongside the pre-existing national state law is not helped by legal pluralism and plural jurisdictions. Such an accommodation contradicts the very foundations of the nation-state and would create societies based on otherness; it goes against what legitimizes law of the nation-state, i.e. the general will. Nevertheless, social diversity requires legal flexibility and political compromise. Still, legal pluralism is not about legal flexibility; rather, it is an attempt to save the nation-state while subsequently and unintentionally undermining the legal foundation of it.

Sharia is a set of moral values; it is a normative way of thinking about right and wrong, and what the good in life is. This can definitely serve as a political principle for finding good laws, but those laws may not be taken for granted as divine and absolute. Such laws are the product of human understanding and reasoning, and they represent the political will of people – not the religious will of God. Because of this, I have argued that this debate is actually about representation, citizenship, political compromise, participation, deliberation, and organization. The call for sharia is actually an expression of political disappointment by Muslims, that the general will does not include them. This might be a difficult suggestion to realize in practice, but I do believe it is the only way in which we can hold on to the nation-state as a form of organizing power. Some argue that we are already living in a post-national era. They are probably right, and the nation-state will not be around eternally. In the meantime, however, we have to address the social problems that exist, and increasingly diverse societies are one such problem. In the case of sharia – apart from the necessary reinterpretation – the best alternative solution is not legal pluralism; it is to encourage political participation and make representation more effective under an equal citizenship.

Notes

[1]. Francois-Cerrah, M. 2014. "Why Banning Sharia Courts Would Harm British Muslim Women", *The Telegraph* (http://www.telegraph.co.uk/women/womens-politics/10973009/Sharia-courts-banwould-harm-British-Muslim-women.html), 17 July.
[2]. Euro-Islam.info, "Islamic Law: Europe's Shari'a Debate" (http://www.euro-islam.info/key-issues/islamic-law/)
[3]. Fournier P. & P. McDougall 2013. "False Jurisdictions? A Revisionist Take on Customary (Religious) Law in Germany", *Texas Intenational Law Journal*, vol. 48 , Spring, pp. 435-463 (http://www.pascalef.com/wp-content/uploads/2013/09/41-Fournier-McDougall-Texas.pdf)
[4]. "Sharia in the West. Whose Law Counts More?", *The Economist* (2010) (http://www.economist.com/node/17249634).
[5]. "The Lebanese Legal System", The Lebanon Report, no 2, Summer, pp. 29-36. (http://www.mallat.com/articles/PDF/TheLebaneseLegalSystem.pdf)
[6]. An-Na'im, A. 2012. *Human Rights and Sharia* (http://www.youtube.com/watch?v=fbvzat5vMyk)
[7]. Bible Gateaway (https://www.biblegateway.com/passage/?searc)
[8]. Leviticus 20 (https://www.biblegateway.com/passage/?search=Leviticus+20)
[9]. Center for Muslim Jewish Engagement (http://www.usc.edu/org/cmje/)
[10]. Hadith, *Center for Muslim Jewish Engagement* (http://www.usc.edu/org/cmje/religious-texts/hadith/)
[11]. Open Letter to Al-Baghdadi (http://www.lettertobaghdadi.com/)

References

Abou El Fadl, K. 2012. *"The Centrality of Sharī'ah to Government and Constitutionalism in Islam"*, in *Constitutionalism in Islamic Countries: Between Upheaval and Continuity,* edited by Rainer Grote and Tilmann J. Röder, pp. 35-61, Oxford: Oxford University Press

Allard-Tremblay, Y. 2013. "Proceduralism, Judicial Review and the Refusal of Royal Assent", *Oxford Journal of Legal Studies*, 33:2, pp. 379-400

An-Na'im, A.A. 2005. "Globalization and Jurisprudence: An Islamic Law Perspective", *Emory Law Journal*, Vol. 54, pp. 25-51

An-Na'im, A.A. 2013. "An inclusive approach to the Mediation of Competing Human Rights Claims", *Constellations*, 20:1, pp. 7-17

Barzilai, G. 2008. "Beyond Relativism: Where Is Political Power in Legal Pluralism?", *Theoretical Inquiries in Law*, 9:2, pp. 395-416

Brown, N.J. 1997. "Sharia and State in the Modern Muslim Middle East", *International Journal of Middle East Studies*, 29:3, pp. 359-376

Brown, N.J. 2002. *Constitutions in a Nonconstitutional World: Arab Basic Laws and the Prospects for Accountable Government*. Albany: State University of New York

Cohen, J. 2010. Rousseau: *A Free Community of Equals.* Oxford: Oxford University Press

Higgins, R.C.A. 2004. *The Moral Limits of Law: Obedience, Respect, and Legitimacy.* Oxford: Oxford University Press

Jackson, S.A. 2006. "Legal Pluralism Between Islam and the Nation-State: Romantic Medievalism or Pragmatic Modernity?", *Fordham International Law Journal,* 30:1, pp. 158-176

Kratochwil, F. 2006. "On Legitimacy", *International Relations*, 20:3, pp. 302-308

Macfarlane, J. 2012. *Islamic Divorce in North America: A Sharia Path in a Secular Society.* Oxford: Oxford University Press

Mallat, C. 1997. "The Lebanese Legal System", *The Lebanon Report*, No. 2, pp. 29-36

Mallat, C. 2009. *Introduction to Middle Eastern Law*. Oxford: Oxford University Press

Pruitt, D.G. and Kim, S.H. 2004. *Social Conflict: Escalation, Stalemate, and Settlement. 3rd ed.*, New York: McGraw-Hill

Putterman, E. 2010. Rousseau, *Law and the Sovereignty of the People.* Cambridge: Cambridge University Press

Raz, J. 1979. *The authority of law: Essays on law and morality.* Revised edition, published to Oxford Scholarship Online, March 2012. Oxford: Oxford University Press

Rousseau, Jean-Jacques. 1762. *Du Contrat Social*, translated by Susan Dunn, 2002, The Social Contract and the First and Second Discourses, pp. 149-254, New Haven: Yale University Press

Sarwar, M.I. 2012. *"Freedom of Religion and Expression: A 'Rule of Law' Perspective"*, in *Islamic Law and International Human Rights Law,* edited by Anver M. Emon, Mark Ellis, and Benjamin Glahn, pp. 247-254, Oxford: Oxford University Press

Shalakany, A.A. 2013. "Islamic Legal Histories", *Berkeley Journal of Middle Eastern & Islamic Law,* 1:1

Tamanaha, B.Z. 2012. "The Rule of Law and Legal Pluralism in Development", in *Legal Pluralism and Development: Scholars and Practitioners in Dialogue,* edited by Brian Z. Tamanaha, Caroline Sage, and Michael Woolcock, pp. 34-49, Cambridge: Cambridge University Press

Twining, W. 2012. "Legal Pluralism 101", in *Legal Pluralism and Development: Scholars and Practitioners in Dialogue,* edited by Brian Z. Tamanaha, Caroline Sage, and Michael Woolcock, pp. 112-128, Cambridge: Cambridge University Press

Woodman, G.R. 1999. "The Idea of Legal Pluralism", in *Legal Pluralism in the Arab World*, edited by Baudouin Dupret, Maurits Berger, and Laila al-Zwaini, pp. 3-20, The Hague: Kluwer Law International

4

Comparing Goals and Aspirations of National vs. Transnational Islamist Movements

JOSEPH KAMINSKI
INTERNATIONAL UNIVERSITY OF SARAJEVO,
BOSNIA AND HERZEGOVINA

Introduction

The previous century saw an Arab world dominated by corrupt monarchies and dictatorships. The nation-state model, as practiced in the Muslim world, failed at many basic functions of what would be considered high quality-governance[1], including the preservation of minority rights. According to Zaid Eyadat,

> Plainly and simply, the regimes and monarchies of old in the region have abysmally failed in producing creative ways for incorporating minorities into the state and the social framework at large. With the emergence of the nation-state came the heavy, top-down approach to solving every undesirable issue, including minority rights. (Eyadat 2013, 735)

As a result of these failures, the late 20th and early 21st centuries have seen a re-emergence in the strength and interest in Islamic-based political movements (Roy 2012 and Eyadat 2013). Despite fears of mixing religion and the state in the West, the Arab and Muslim world in general have been more accepting of this taboo idea in the minds of liberals. "While the West is inherently suspicious of the rise of Islam as a political force, Arabs are much more diverse in their political attitudes" (Eyadat 2013, 734). This article looks to show some similarities and differences between national and transnational Islamist movements in regards to tolerance, religious freedom, and the use of violence.

I will look in greater detail at the examples of Tunisia's Ennahda Movement, the Muslim Brotherhood in Egypt, and Hamas as national-based Islamist movements in the next section. Following a discussion of national Islamist movements, I will look at transnational Islamist movements. I will look at the cases of al-Qaeda and ISIS as examples of contemporary transnational Islamist movements. The last section will look at the hybrid case of Hezbollah.

National-based Islamist Movements

Perhaps one of the most successful current Islamist movements in Africa, in terms of sustained political power and influence, is Tunisia's Ennahda Movement. Ennahda emerged under the name *Ḥarakat al-Ittijāh al-Islāmī*, or "The Movement of Islamic Tendency," in 1981. It changed its name in 1989 to *Ḥarakat an-Nahḍah*. Ennahda gained inspiration from the Iranian Revolution in 1979 (despite Tunisia being almost 100% Sunni), the Egyptian Muslim Brotherhood, and the ideas of Hasan al-Banna (Wright 2001 and Lewis 2011).

While the original Ennahda movement in the 1980s was more extremist-oriented, they changed their course in more recent times. According to Aiden Lewis, "Aligned with more extreme Islamist movements elsewhere in the Arab world in the 1980s, Mr[.] Ghannouchi and other Ennahda leaders now like to compare Ennahda to the Justice and Development Party (AKP) in Turkey" (Lewis 2011). Ghannouchi sees similarities in the way Islam undergirds both Turkish and Tunisian society. Both nations have almost unanimous Muslim populations and both nations each possess one of the most revered Islamic Holy Sites in the world; the *Hagia Sofia* in Istanbul, Turkey, and the Great Mosque of Kairouan in Kairouan, Tunisia.

After Ennahda gained power following the overthrow of the enormously unpopular autocrat Zine El Abidine Ben Ali, out of pragmatic interests they incorporated some elements of the previous regime into the new government. In the words of Ennahda's leader and founder, Rachid al Ghannouchi, "Power-Sharing in a Muslim or Non-Muslim environment becomes a necessity in order to lay the foundations of the social order" (Ghannouchi 1998, 273). Ennahda's leadership recognised that this would assist in the transition to power. According to Longo:

In fact, when Nida was formed after the 2011 revolution, al-Nahda has integrated several members of the former regime into its ranks to secure them a role in the aftermath of revolution and strengthen its position vis-à-vis other political forces. This is the case of Habib Essid, long-standing politician during the 1990s, who was appointed Minister of the Interior during the transitional phase led by Mabazaa and Essebsi, and then advisor of the Prime Minister during the first al-Nahda's government led by Hamadi Jebali. (Longo 2014)

Flexibility was a concern of Ennahda from the moment it came to power. Ghannouchi himself states, "Realism and flexibility are amongst the most important features of Islamic methodology" (Ghannouchi 1998, 272). Ghannouchi recognises that different historical geo-political circumstances require different ways of governing a state. One cannot simply graft an 8th century-style caliphate in a 21st century world.

Once in power, Ennahda minimised some of the more controversial Islamist elements of their constitution. This action actually strengthened its position against other secular parties. "Now that the new Constitution has been adopted, and it is less 'Islamic' than any expectation, paradoxically the anti-Islamist front is weaker than ever and has lost its glue" (Longo 2014). Ghannouchi has articulated that the principles of justice articulated in the Quran ought to serve as the foundation and basis of what is constitutive of justice. "Ghannushi maintains that re-reading of the authoritative texts of the Quran and Hadith is governed by certain principles that have become the basis for determining what is acceptable or otherwise in the modern period, a key one of which is 'justice' ('*adl*)" (Saeed 1999, 312). Ultimately justice is found within the Quran the proper interpretation and implementation of the sharia. However, as a realist, Ghannouchi and Ennahda recognize the necessity of pragmatically reaching their goals, rather than using violence like transnational groups do.

The Egyptian Muslim Brotherhood [Egyptian MB] is another example of a national-based Islamist movement (Rubin 2010a and Rubin 2010b). While the general Muslim Brotherhood movement has spread to other nations, its overall agenda is based with a pre-existing national setting; each individual MB movement sought political power *within* an existing demarcated territory. According to Rubin, "The Brotherhoods in each country are independent of each other; they usually do not use terrorism; they often follow different policies adapted to their surroundings; and they often try to avoid publicity" (Rubin 2010b, 1). These individual national MB movements did not seek to annex/commandeer land the same way Al Qaeda sought to, and ISIS actually has. This is why this article argues the case of the Egyptian Muslim

Brotherhood is an example of a national-based Islamist movement.

The Egyptian MB's roots can be traced back to Hasan al-Banna in 1928. His movement grew steadily during the 1930s and into the 1940s (Soage and Franganillo 2010). It is widely believed that the Egyptian monarchy had an interest in his death. In 1948, rumours of a Brotherhood-led coup on Mahmoud Fahmi an-Nukrashi Pasha, the second Egyptian Prime Minister of the Kingdom of Egypt, emerged (Hussain 2010). Al-Banna was eventually killed in 1949. In the 1950s, Nasser continued efforts to limit the influence of the Egyptian MB, but by this point, the movement had established firm roots in Egyptian society.

> The Ikhwan [brotherhood] attached itself to, and built strategic relations with mosques, welfare associations and neighbourhood groups, whilst seeking to influence existing activists with its revolutionary ideas. By joining local cells, members could access a well-established and well-resourced community of activists who would help them in all aspects of their lives. (Hussain 2010, 2)

In the 1960s, the Egyptian MB's most popular figure was Sayyid Qutb. Qutb did not call for global jihad; rather, he called for a refocusing of Islamic values in already-existing Muslim societies (Rubin 2010a). In *Milestones*, Qutb's main concern was the growing Jahiliyyah, or state of barbarous ignorance, that he feared Muslims in Muslim lands were returning to via infatuation with the immoral elements of western culture. According to Qutb:

> We are also surrounded by Jahiliyyah today, which is of the same nature as it was during the first period of Islam, perhaps a little deeper. Our whole environment, people's beliefs and ideas, habits and art, rules and laws-is Jahiliyyah, even to the extent that what we consider to be Islamic culture, Islamic sources, Islamic philosophy and Islamic thought are also constructs of Jahiliyyah! (Qutb 2007, 6)

The theme of returning to a more pure state of Islamic discourse and would continue to be influential into the 21st century, and was central in the 2012 Mohammed Morsi presidential platform. Morsi's agenda sought to reintroduce Islam into the political apparatus. He was deeply concerned with issues of religious rights and freedoms among minorities. In an address as president given in Tahrir Square, as reported by *the Guardian*, he states:

> I call upon you to begin this renaissance project. We

> Egyptians, Muslims and Christians, are harbingers of development and civilisation and we will remain so. We will meet the trials and schemes which are aimed at undermining our resolve and national unity as we did during the revolution. I am determined with you to astound the world with the Egyptian revival that realises prosperity, dignity and stability. I am determined, with your help, to build a new Egypt, a civil state, which is democratically constituted. All my energies will be devoted to this great project. I will work to preserve Egypt's national interests on all fronts, Arab and African, regional and international. (Mohammed Morsi, Address at Tahrir Square, 2012)

The civil state envisioned by the new leadership, at the least on paper, made clear their desires to encourage diversity and multiculturalism. Despite some statements made by the Muslim Brotherhood in 2013 that seemed antithetical to women's rights, Morsi's regime allowed for women to participate in their political movement. According to Pakinam El-Sharkawy, one of Morsi's female political advisors:

> The Brotherhood, she emphasised, does not speak for the president; he has resigned from the Brotherhood but remains a member of its political party. "Does any statement issued by any political party or group represent the presidency?" she asked. "It's not the presidency's institution, and it's not an official entity." (Kirkpatrick and Sheikh, 14 March, 2013)

The Morsi-led Egyptian Muslim Brotherhood sought to keep its domestic politics within its own borders; it did not seek to export them to other places. Morsi was much more interested in engaging with traditional Islamist allies in terms of foreign policy than pervious regimes; however, he did not seek to expand his domain of rule or territory, similar to the aims of the Ennahda Movement in Tunisia.

Not all national-based islamist movements renounce violence

One cannot simply argue that all national-based Islamist movements are opposed to the use of violence; this article argues that there is a tendency within *most* national Islamist movements to, at the least, renounce violence as a means to achieving political goals. The most obvious counter-example is that of Hamas in Gaza.

The way violence is utilised in the case of Hamas is different than the cases of ISIS and Al Qaeda. While ISIS and Al Qaeda both are not representatives of any single territory such as Hamas, ISIS and Al Qaeda tend to use violence against whomever they feel is a threat to their interests; Hamas' violence is targeted at solely a specific entity: Israel. "By the early 1990's, it no longer sought to antagonise others as readily as in the past" (Hroub 2000, 51). Hamas differentiated that its principal enemy was Israel and not Western states that supported it. While Hamas still opposed western support of Israel, they did not seek to wage Jihad on the West as did/does al-Qaeda and ISIS.

Considering levels of violence seen during Israel's 2014 *Operation Protective Edge*, the situation between Gaza and Israel is by all reasonable standards an ongoing civil war. Israel's naval blockade of the waters off the coast of Gaza, by UN standards, would be an open declaration of war if Gaza was formally recognised as an autonomous nation-state.[2] "The act of initiating a blockade is tantamount to an act of war, and is one of the enumerated specific acts of aggression that appears in the [UN] General Assembly's consensus definition of Aggression adopted on 14 December 1974" (Kraska 2010, 379-380). As Gaza continues to lack the autonomy of a legally recognised state, it is likely to continue to use violence. When states feel in a corner with 'nothing to lose,' they are more likely to engage in violence, as opposed to when they do feel they have some tangible benefit to lose (Mecham 2006). Like any state or movement, national or transnational, when one feels threatened, they are more likely to respond with violence.

Transnational Islamist movements

Transnational Islamist movements are those movements that do not limit themselves to any specific national boundary or government, and seek to impose their worldview on an area not confined to any one particular nation-state's legally demarcated territorial borders. The transition from a national to transitional movement is often a tactical choice on part of the movement. This is to say a movement can start of as a national movement and evolve into a transnational movement. "For many Islamist organisations, the evolution from a national to a transnational organisation is primarily the result of tactical rather than strategic choices designed to ensure the survival and legitimacy of the movement" (Mecham 2006, 3). Such movements consist primarily of an ethnically homogenous population who perceive themselves as oppressed by a foreign power or foreign powers with respect to territory (Burroughs-Johnson 2013). According to Quinn Mecham, there are three specific conditions that cause Islamist movements tend to become 'transnational.' Understanding these conditions can shed light on why some of these transnational movements become what they do. Mecham states:

> In particular, Islamist movements are likely to become increasingly transnational under three principal conditions: a) when members of the domestic Islamist movement become linked to participation in external conflicts through training activities; b) when the movement's funding is transnational and the funding party creates organisational incentives for transnational ties; and c) when geographic resources necessary for sustained mobilisation in repressive contexts become external to state boundaries. (Mecham 2006, 2)

Unlike national-based Islamist movements such as *Ennahda* in Tunisia and the Muslim Brotherhood-led Egyptian state in 2012, transnational Islamist movements by nature tend to exist more at the fringes of political society. Such groups generally lack direct access to national political processes; as a result of this exclusion, often such movements have little to no interest in cooperating and making concessions to any formal state-led entity.

> [I]f Islamist groups are not incorporated into domestic political processes but instead are forcibly repressed by the state, they may become transnational organisations, which are extremely difficult to control. Because transnational groups do not respond well to domestic policies, they are less likely to change in response to political incentives. (Mecham 2006, 5)

Transnational Islamist movements, by nature, tend to vacillate between violence and non-violence, depending on external circumstances. At times such movements are focused more on domestic issues, while at other times these same movements are much more concerned with global issues.

With regards to Al Qaeda, which literally means, 'the base' in Arabic, the group from its beginnings was a transnational Islamist organisation. Created in the late 1980s and largely funded by a wealthy Saudi national, Osama Bin Laden, Al Qaeda from its very beginning were dedicated to the creation of a global caliphate and the use of violence of unprecedented scales to achieve their ends (Moghadam 2010). They also sought to encourage participation in their movement from Muslims (Sunni, of course) from all over the world. In their own words, "We wish especially to reach out to our brothers and sisters in Muslim societies. We say to you forthrightly: We are not enemies, but friends. We must not be enemies" (Ibrahim 2007, 18).

While Al Qaeda were most certainly a transnational Islamist movement, their movement actually lacks much of what would be traditionally considered a 'political apparatus.' Al Qaeda does not have legislators, politicians, courts, or even clearly demarcated constitutional codes. Rather, Al Qaeda's 'doctrine' is largely a hodgepodge of Quranic interpretations and fatwas from individuals often not qualified to issue them, and the formal execution of 'commands and rulings' are not clearly defined or understood. If one breaks an Al Qaeda decree within the organisation, there is no recognisable, formal 'legal or governing body' that can be immediately pointed to as the entity that will carry out the punishment. A similar reality is emerging with the most recent transnational Islamist movement to come into public view: ISIS.

As mentioned in the previous paragraph, at the core of Al Qaeda's mission is to engage in violence. With regards to violence against the West, one Al Qaeda essay states:

> The ruling to kill the Americans and their allies—civilians and military—is an individual obligation incumbent upon every Muslim who can do it and in any country—this until the Aqsa Mosque [Jerusalem] and the Holy Mosque [Mecca] are liberated from their grip, and until their armies withdraw from all lands of Islam, defeated, shattered, and unable to threaten any Muslim. (Ibrahim 2000, 13)

One can see that these demands are quite broad. While they speak of the 'liberation' of al-Aqsa and the Holy Mosque of Mecca, they do not actually define what this means. In order for these Mosques to be 'properly liberated,' who must be in control and how must they operate? None of these specific questions are directly addressed. The same can be said of the vague demand that Americans must be killed until they are 'shattered, and unable to threaten any Muslims.' This is another non-quantifiable demand. Such broad ideological demands lacking actual concreteness seem to be a common theme with many transnational Islamist movements.

Despite the lack of concreteness in many terms used, one thing that is clear in the case of al-Qaeda is a desire to see the fall of the West. According to the well-known, high-ranking al-Qaeda operative Saif al-Adel's document, "al-Qaeda's Strategy to the Year 2020," the American economic system will eventually collapse by 2020 due to the numerous military engagements across the globe which will eventually lead to a Jihad led by Al Qaeda, and ultimately a Wahhābi Caliphate that will rule over the world (Atwan 2006). The explicit desire for the destruction of other nation-states and their ways of life are a major difference between national and transnational Islamist movements.

Beginning in 2014, Al Qaeda had taken a backseat to a new transnational

Islamist movement that has already changed its name three times. Originally the Islamic State of Iraq and the Levant (ISIL) and the Islamic State of Iraq and Syria (ISIS), the movement now simply goes by the name IS, or the Islamic State.[3] On the seriousness of the global threat posed by the Islamic State, British Prime Minister David Cameron states, "We face in Isil [ISIS] a new threat that is single-minded, determined and unflinching in pursuit of its objectives" (Khomami 8/16/2014). ISIS has been able to amalgamate a bizarre coalition against it, including the US, Great Britain, the current Iraqi government, the Assad Regime, the moderate Syrian rebels, Kurds, and even Iran. The Islamic State represents an amalgamation of various Al Qaeda-linked groups into one 'coherent' entity that has already declared itself a Caliphate, something Al Qaeda never even tried to do, with its leader being Abu-Bakr al-Baghdadi, a shadowy figure whose past is almost entirely unknown.

As this article is being prepared, much mystery still surrounds ISIS. One thing is clear thus far: they have taken violence to a new level of theatrical production that even trumps Al Qaeda. Within a period of weeks during the summer of 2014, two American reporters, Steven Sotloff and James Foley, and British aid worker David Haines, were barbarically beheaded in gruesome public videos which were clearly pre-meditated and meticulously choreographed. ISIS currently is active in its efforts to conquer new territories. They have large areas of territory under their control in northern Iraq, and have even made it across the border into Syria. At this point, it is impossible to evaluate the bureaucratic organisation within ISIS due to the secrecy of the organisation itself and the limited scholarly research on the topic at the time this article is being written. However, considering the appointment of an all-powerful Caliph, it is reasonable to assume that ISIS internally is organised around charismatic and traditional models of authority, as opposed to rational-legal models as outlined by Max Weber in his studies of bureaucracy in *Politics as a Vocation* (Weber 1946).

Hezbollah, the hybrid case

This final section will briefly look at Hezbollah. Hezbollah is perhaps the best example of what one might consider a hybrid movement that can be placed somewhere on the continuum between a national and transnational movement. While they are technically a political party based in Lebanon, they have been active in other, external, regional affairs for over 30 years. They were the main combatants in recent wars with Israel and most recently have offered military support to Bashar al-Assad's regime in the current Syrian civil war. Unlike national-based movements, they are not wholly autonomous; they are closely connected to, and financed by, the Iranian government and other private entities (Levitt 2013).

Interestingly, they incorporate elements of both types of movements discussed. Like national-based Islamist movements, Hezbollah does not exist on the fringes of society; they have a wide following in Shi'a dominated parts of Lebanon. They also have a more recognisable formal internal organisational structure that has been studied extensively (Norton 2014). Within Hezbollah, there are numerous councils and organisations. Hezbollah also has an extensive propaganda apparatus, including its own television station, *al Manar*, which can be viewed on regular cable throughout Lebanon.

However, like a transnational Islamist movement, Hezbollah operates in a much wider global context than just within the Lebanese borders. They do utilise violence, and they often engage in violent rhetoric denouncing Zionism, the West, and other Sunni groups, specifically those believe to be connected to the Saudi regime (Levitt 2013 and Norton 2014). When politically expedient, they renounce violence and call for reconciliation between the different religious sects within Lebanon, however, when it is politically expedient, they call for violence against self-described 'Zionist-Wahhābi collaborators.'

Their current leader, Sheikh Hasan Nasrallah, took over the position of Secretary General of the group in 1992 following the assassination of Abbas al-Musawi by Israeli Defense Forces. Nasrallah's power derives from all three sources of authority under the Weberian model. It derives from rational-legal authority, based on the powers given to him within the official charter and rather developed legalistic framework of the party; it derives from charismatic authority, based on his popularity gained via fighting in multiple wars and skirmishes against Israel; and it derives from traditional authority, based on the fact that he is a *Sayyid*, or believed to be a direct descendent of the Prophet Mohammed, through his grandson, Ali, thus automatically granting him a higher status within Shi'a society than other people.

Conclusion

Political Movements within the Islamic discourse have each made efforts to address issues such as 'rights and freedoms' in their own ways. In recent years, there has been a great deal of writing on the topic of individual rights. According to Tariq Ramadan:

> There can be no ambiguity about the ethical orientation that Islam provides: 'We have conferred dignity on human being' – a principle that applies to all humans, women and men, rich and poor, black and white, Muslim or not. It is the primary, fundamental principle of social justice that, in practice, rests on

two prerequisites: equal rights and equal opportunities. (Ramadan 2012, 125)

This article sought to show some clear differences and themes between national and transnational Islamist movements. One thing that differentiates national-based Islamist movements from transnational-based Islamist movements is each movement's approach to diverse political attitudes and differing religious value systems.

Islamist movements that operate within existing national borders tend to be accommodating to diverse populations, sometimes garnering support from secularists. According to Eyadat, "Secularists cling to their principles, fearing the rise of an extreme theocracy like Iran, but an increasing amount of support is espoused for moderate Islamic movements, like the Muslim Brotherhood in Egypt or *Ennahda* in Tunisia, as their framework allows for a reconciliation of religious beliefs and political inclusion" (Eyadat 2013, 734). National Islamist movements are more formally organised internally and have bureaucratic structures based primarily on rational-legal authority. They do not seek to annex/expand territorially, and they exist within the mainstream of local politics.

Transnational Islamist movements often do not have a clear organisational/ bureaucratic structure; the policy making process is vague and opaque. Oftentimes they completely lack commonly found institutions within any normally functioning modern bureaucratic entity. These movements generally call for violence and conquest, often seeking to constantly extend their territorial boundaries. Usually the violence is coupled with brutally, well-choreographed, videotaped executions of non-combatants. They generally exist at the fringes of political society. People ought to be aware of these important differences before they immediately connect the word 'Islamism' immediately to 9/11 and suicide bombings.

Notes

[1] For a more detailed discussion of the idea of good governance, see Rothstein, Bo. (2011). *The Quality of Government: Corruption, Social Trust, and Inequality in International Perspective.* Chicago, IL: University of Chicago Press.
[2] Article 3(c), UNGA Res. 3314, 14 December 1974.
[3] For the sake of clarity, this article will address the Islamic State, or IS, as 'ISIS.'

References

Atwan, Abdel Bari. (2006). *The Secret History of Al Qaeda*. Berkeley, CA: University of California Press.

Burroughs-Johnson, Andrew. (2013). "Transnational Irish and Islamic Movements." *E-International Relations*. http://www.e-ir.info/2013/05/03/transnational-irish-and-islamic-movements/

Eyadat, Zaid. (2013). "Fiqh Al-Aqalliyyaˆt and the Arab Spring: Modern Islamic Theorizing." *Philosophy & Social Criticism,* 39(8): 733-753.

Ghannouchi, R. (1998). "The Participation of Islamists in a Non-Islamic Government," in C. Kurzman (Ed.), *Liberal Islam: A Sourcebook*. New York: Oxford Press. pp 271-278.

Hroub, Khaled. (2000). *Hamas: Political Thought and Practice*. Washington D.C.: Institute for Palestinian Studies.

Hussain, G. (2010). *"A Short History of Islamism" (Concept Series)*. London: Quilliam.

Ibrahim, Raymond. (2000). *The Al Qaeda Reader*. New York: Broadway Books.

Kirkpatrick, D. and El Sheikh, M. "Muslim Brotherhood's Statement on Women Stirs Liberals' Fears," *New York Times*, 14 March, 2013. http://www.nytimes.com/2013/03/15/world/middleeast/muslim-brotherhoods-words-on-women-stir-liberal-fears.html?_r=0

Khomami, N. "Cameron Urges Swift Action Against ISIS," *The Guardian*. 16, August 2014. http://www.theguardian.com/world/2014/aug/16/cameron-isis-uk-terror-threat

Kraska, James (2010). "Rule Selection in the Case of Israel's Naval Blockade of Gaza: Law of Naval Warfare of Law of the Sea?," in, *Schmitt, Arimatsu, and McCormack (Eds.), Yearbook of International Humanitarian Law - 2010: 2010. Volume 1*. The Hague, Netherlands: T.M.C Asher Press. pp. 367-396.

Levitt, M. (2013). *Hezbollah: The Global Footprint of Lebanon's Party of God*. Washington DC: Georgetown University Press.

Lewis, A. "Profile: Tunisia's Ennahda Party," *BBC News,* 25 October, 2011. http://www.bbc.co.uk/news/world-africa-15442859

Longo, Pietro. (2014). "Tunisia's Upcoming Election amid Strategic Reshaping of Coalitions." *E-International Relations.* http://www.e-ir.info/2014/08/05/tunisias-upcoming-elections-reshaping-of-coalitions/

Mecham, Quinn. (2006). "Why Do Islamist Groups Become Transnational and Violent?" *MIT Center for International Studies Audit of the Conventional Wisdom,* 06-11.

Moghadam, A. (2008). *The Globalization of Martyrdom: Al Qaeda, Salafi Jihad, and the Diffusion of Suicide Attacks.* Baltimore: Johns Hopkins University.

Morsi, M. (2012) "I have today become president of all Egyptians," translated into English by, The Muslim Brotherhood, reported in *The Guardian,* 25 June, 2012. Accessed online at http://www.theguardian.com/commentisfree/2012/jun/25/president-egyptians-mohamed-morsi

Norton, R. (2014) *Hezbollah: A Short History.* Princeton, NJ: Princeton University Press.

Qutb, Sayyid. (2007). *Milestones.* Damascus, Syria: Kazi Publishers.

Ramadan, Tariq. (2012). *The Arab Awakening: Islam and the New Middle East.* London: Allen Lane.

Roy, Oliver. (2004). *Globalized Islam: The Search for a New Ummah.* New York:. Columbia University Press.

Rubin, Barry. (2010a). "An Introduction to Assessing Contemporary Islamism," in B. Rubin (ed.), *A Guide to Global Islamist Movements.* New York: M.E. Sharpe Publishing.

Rubin, Barry. (2010b). "Comparing the Three Muslim Brotherhoods," in B. Rubin (ed.), *The Muslim Brotherhood: The Organizational Policies of a Global Islamist Movement.* New York: Palgrave MacMillan. Pp 1-18.

Saeed, Abdullah. (1999). "Rethinking citizenship Rights of Non-Muslims in an Islamic State: Rashid al Ghannushi's contribution to the evolving debate." *Islam and Christian Muslim Relations.* 10(3): 307-323.

Soage, A. and Franganillo, J.F. (2010) "The Muslim Brothers in Egypt," in B. Rubin (ed.), *The Muslim Brotherhood: The Organizational Policies of a Global Islamist Movement.* New York: Palgrave MacMillan. Pp. 39-55.

Weber, Max. (1946). "Politics as a Vocation," in Garth and Mills (Eds.), *Essays in Sociology.* New York: Macmillan. Pp. 25-46.

Wright, R. (2001). *Sacred Rage.* New York: Simon and Schuster.

5

The Islamic State and the Arab Tribes in Eastern Syria

HAIAN DUKHAN
UNIVERSITY OF SAINT ANDREWS,SCOTLAND (UK)

SINAN HAWAT
INDEPENDENT RESEARCHER

Introduction

In a recent book written by Akbar Ahmed titled *The Thistle and the Drone: How America's War on Terror Became a Global War on Tribal Islam* (Ruthven, 2013), the author explained how tribal identity was a crucial factor in the recruitment of the planes' hijackers during the events of 9/11. "Bin Laden," he states, "was joined in his movement primarily by his fellow Yemeni tribesmen," ten of whom came from the Asir tribes, including Ghamed, Zahran, and Bani Shahr (Ahmed, 2013). Tribal groups that live on the borders between states were often overlooked by many in the discussion about Islamic extremists and their relationship to other groups. These groups forge tight relations with other militant Islamist groups, providing them with protection and support. One can see that in many places, such as Afghanistan, Iraq, and recently Syria. In the former, al-Qaeda members received the protection and support from local tribal members of the Mehsud and Wazir tribes, many of whom had been serving with the Taliban in the country since the 1990s (Gunaratna & Nielsen, 2008). In Iraq, after the American invasion, al-Qaeda (Dawlat al-'Iraq al-Islāmīyah, "Islamic State of Iraq," ISI)[1] has existed in the eastern part of Syria – where the desert and the tribes straddle the border with Iraq – for almost a decade (Abdul-Ahad, 2012). When the Syrian uprising started, ISI sent Syrian jihadists who were already in Iraq, in addition to Iraqi experts in guerrilla warfare who sneaked into the country. It is clear by this pattern of behaviour that al-Qaeda-affiliated groups seek safe haven in border regions, typically inhabited by local tribes, where the prevailing sentiment is a strong apathy toward the state. Such example regions are Waziristan in Pakistan, the province of Shabwa in Yemen, the province of al-Anbar in Iraq, and recently the Syrian dry Steppe.

By March 2013, fighters of ISI were able to take the city of Raqqa, one of Syria's heavily tribal regions. After a few weeks of capturing the city, the group released a video that showed what it called swearing an oath of allegiance to the state by more than a *"dozen tribes in the province of Raqqa"* (أبو أمل الشمري , 2013). As ISIS[2] continued its march in Deir ez-Zor and seized control of its towns and villages, tribal leaders started issuing statements of loyalty to the Islamic state. This was the beginning of an allegiance of one tribe after the other in the whole Syrian Steppe. This article seeks to examine the factors influencing the relationship between ISIS and the tribal community east of Syria. It argues that shared economic and political interests and common foes (mainly Bashar al-Assad's regime) are enabling the group to build foundations within the tribal community of Syria. It ends by concluding that the longer ISIS keeps control of Syrian territory from its de facto capital in Raqqa, the more deeply embedded it will be within the tribal community of Syria, which will complicate US efforts to fight the group because, as airstrikes expand, ISIS will dig into civilian areas and more people of the tribal community will be killed.

How it all started

The central element in tribal formation is the establishment of kinship groups. Each member of the group is responsible for each and every other member and the group's 'acts' are called "collective action" (Salzman, 2008). When attacked, group members are obliged to unite to defend themselves; when members sustain injury or loss, group members unite to gain compensation or seek vengeance. When applying these dynamics to the tribal community of Syria, we will be able to understand that the taking up of arms by the Syrian tribes against the Syrian regime came as a response to the regime's violence (Dukhan, 2014). This behaviour corresponds with the concept of *intiqaam*, which means revenge for real or perceived offenses committed against one's kin. Members of the Arab tribes in Syria are bound by honour to take vengeance upon the aggressor, which, in this case, are the Syrian security forces who are deemed hostile towards the members of the tribe.

As the conflict escalated, tribal militias composed of many Syrian army defectors were formed in different parts of the Syrian Steppe, which constitutes 55% of Syrian land. Their mobility, combined with their loyalty to their kin groups and their military capacity due to the arms bought during the

American invasion of Iraq and the chaos that followed it, gave them the ability to drive the Syrian regime army out of many of their villages and towns. Not all tribes fought against the regime, however. Some tribal leaders who have close links to the security services in Syria have remained loyal to the regime.[3] At a later stage, these militias have pursued longstanding rivalries between themselves by aligning with ISIS or its adversaries – including the Assad regime and al-Qaeda affiliate Jabhat al-Nusra (JN) – for controlling oil fields or gaining more war plunder. Despite ISIS's strict adherence to Islamic law, which is unwelcomed by the more moderate tribal society, ISIS was able to get more tribes to stand by its side against Jabhat al-Nusra. During their conflict over the territories of the Syrian Steppe, both groups formed alliances with certain tribes, creating a coalition of tribes which routinely issue statements of threat to opposing tribes. By capturing Jabhat al-Nusra's nerve-centre in Deir ez Zor, if not all of Syria, Shuhail,[4] it could be said that ISIS has won the tribal warfare that it waged against JN for a few months over the Syrian Steppe. With these alliances of convenience with the tribes, ISIS has bolstered its social control not only with direct coercion or with mass expulsion of uncooperative tribes, but also by restoration of public services and other manifestations of the central state (Sayigh, 2014).

Factors influencing the alliance of convenience between ISIS and the tribes of the Syrian Steppe

The complex nature of the relation between the tribes in Syria and ISIS can be explained through three main arguments. The first argument emphasises the rational factors that govern this relationship. These factors include economic benefits and protection. The second argument highlights the fear factor, skilfully exploited and mastered by ISIS. The last argument focuses on the grievances, which make the tribes accept or tolerate ISIS in the face of a common enemy.

To understand the rational argument that explains the allegiances of some tribes to ISIS, one needs to consider the development of events not only since the beginning of the uprising in Syria, but also before it. During the rule of Hafez al-Assad, tribes were co-opted and used as tools for indirect rule through the use of official appointment and subsidiaries (Dukhan, 2014). They were used to check the expansion of Muslim Brotherhood in Hama and the Kurds in the North Eastern part of the country. Tribes were part of the formidable populist powers that shored up the regime. However, after opening the economy to the world market, the Ba'athist ideology was abandoned and the presence of the state and its services started to diminish among tribal communities in the peripheries (Hinnebusch, 2012). In Syria, ISIS attempted to fill the gap formed by the withdrawal of the state. It provided an alternative structure of clientelism and patronage. It is thought that ISIS co-opts tribes and supports some of their leaders by providing them with the opportunity to be influential in return for allegiance (Salama, 2014). This explains the fact that many of the tribes who were previously loyal to the Syrian regime in exchange for little power have switched their allegiance and opted to support ISIS. Moreover, ISIS's ability to gain substantial funding after controlling large reserves of oil and gas in Syria has enabled it to provide services and start development projects, such as fixing bridges, providing clean water, and establishing irrigation projects (Hassan, 2014). During Bashar al-Assad's reign, the tribes in al-Badia have been marginalized and impoverished. They saw that the natural resources in their region are being siphoned off by the president, his grandiose projects, and the elite, and not in the interests of their local communities. When trying to protest against those policies, Bashar al-Assad used massive force against them. The Syrian regime's tyranny forced many tribes to accept that ISIS might equally distribute their wealth over Bashar al-Assad, who has not acknowledged their demands and forced them to take up arms.

Other tribes that refuse to be co-opted by ISIS would be intimidated to do so. This leads us to the fear argument, which attempts to explain some aspects of the relation between ISIS and the tribes. The former uses fear as a weapon of war. In this regard, Dr. Fawaz Gerges (2014), from the London School of Economics, explains that while brutality and savagery might seem senseless to the vast majority of civilised human beings, they constitute a rational and conscious choice that impress and co-opt new recruits. Indeed, publishing videos of atrocities such as decapitation or crucifixion of the members of the Shaitat clan that tried to revolt against ISIS[5] aims to demonstrate the invincibility and ruthlessness of the militia and to spread fear among its enemy. It subtly invites recruits either to choose the winning horse or die.

The theological pretext that justifies the harsh conduct of ISIS is derived from al-Hiraba law, which is a Muslim law concerning organized crime and highway robbery (Legal Reference, 2014). This law depends on a particular verse in Quran that rules harsh punishment against rebels who rage war against the state or conduct armed robbery. The punishment is not only killing, but also crucifixion and amputation. Portraying itself as a state, ISIS uses this verse and considers all those who stand against its goal as conspirators liable to be treated according to it. ISIS is very keen to spread this message everywhere; hence the web is replete with gruesome images and videos of execution and crucifixion taking place in areas controlled by ISIS. While discussing terror techniques, it is worth noting that these are by no means exclusive to the Islamic State. Amputation was used extensively in many civil wars, such as in Sierra Leone. However, ISIS has clearly excelled in spreading its messages of terror using high-tech means and cutting-edge technology, making these techniques more useful.

The final group of factors that can explain the relation between ISIS and the tribal society in Syria is the context of civil war and the grievances it produces. These grievances endured by the tribes may well explain their inclination to tolerate – or even cooperate with – ISIS. The latter capitalises on these grievances to gain recruitment and allegiance.

Grievance has played an important role in the engagement of tribes in the Syrian uprising as it has provided the necessary push for public mobilisation. Many writers question how a society becomes engaged in rebellion against a government. Some writers, such as Paul Collier (2000), believe that there must be an economic incentive that convinces people to take part in a rebellion. Grievances according to such writers are not enough to mobilise people to rebel. In a sense, justice and relief from grievance are considered to be public goods which suffer from the problem of free-riding, in which individuals are reluctant to act, considering the high cost of participation, and they tend to wait for others to act to benefit from them once successful. This problem sabotages political collective action in dictatorships where the cost of participating in a rebellion is very high (such as being jailed or even killed). In such conditions, people tend to be reluctant to initiate a rebellion because the rational choice for an individual is not to put oneself in danger, to wait for the movement to succeed, and then to benefit from the outcome. On this basis, Collier argues that there must be an economic benefit that convinces people to engage in a rebellion, otherwise rebellion will not take place. However, the tribal society provides a counterargument to Collier's ideas as kinship, which is the dominant idiom of organisation for tribes, motivates individuals to mobilise in defence of their fellow tribe members. Tribal bonds between the families of the Syrian Steppe have been very important in organising the first protests in the region (Dukhan, 2014).

The Syrian regime intentionally targeted community leaders who expressed views against the regime. While this meant to terrorise the society and show the government's ruthless face, it has fanned the flames of opposition and resistance. One of the humiliating techniques used is arresting a community leader or an opposition public figure and making them confess on TV about their alleged crimes, or forcing them to announce their detachment from the opposition. An example of this practice is the arrest of Nawaf al-Bashir, the chief of the al-Bagara tribe. His arrest and humiliation have created uproar within the tribal society. With all these grievances, many tribal leaders may find ISIS a natural reaction to the brutality of the regime, or less harmful than it, at least. Indeed, in an interview with one of the most influential tribal leaders in Iraq, Sheikh Hatem al-Suleiman downplayed the role of ISIS and considered the Iraqi government to be more dangerous (Ali, 2014). ISIS and similar militias excel in the presence of grievances because they provide them with the most needed legitimacy.

Conclusion

The article has laid some of the factors that influence the relationship between ISIS and the tribal community in Syria. Identifying these factors plays an important role in predicting the outcomes of efforts to counter ISIS in the region. This is particularly relevant to the coalition attacks on ISIS both in Syria and Iraq.

Initially, by increasing outreach to the local tribes, ISIS plays a similar role to the 'populist' authoritarian regime of Hafez al-Assad. While the organisation is using coercive means of power towards the tribes, it is also providing them with the basic needs which make them dependent on it as a distributive agency. Additionally, ISIS can be seen as the outcome of the Sunni alienation in the region. According to Hassan (2014), Sunnis, although the majority, act as a minority in the region: constantly feeling insecure, paranoid, and under siege. In this context, ISIS has become appealing to many tribes sharing the Sunni grievances. ISIS can be perceived by the tribes simply as an ally of necessity, essential for responding to the aggressions of a sectarian government perceived as an Iranian-backed occupation force (Harling, 2014).

Now with the coalition waging a war on ISIS and other Islamist groups, it seems that this will further alienate the Sunni communities in the peripheries and inevitably provide ISIS with the needed legitimacy. By overlooking the regime of Bashar al-Assad, which has ignited the Syrian uprising and led to the death of thousands of Syrians in Syria generally and the Syrian Steppe particularly, the air strikes leave the local people in no doubt about the international coalition's indifference to their welfare or survival. Achieving the coalition's objective of destroying ISIS will depend on not only hitting the right targets at the right time, but reaching out to Arab tribes as well (Tabler, 2014). It is unlikely that the tribes will cooperate with the coalition against ISIS rule because the tribes are fearful of the return of a vengeful regime.

Notes

[1] The group had a number of different names. In 2004, the group leader Abu Musab al-Zarqawi swore loyalty to Osama bin Laden. On 13 October 2006, the establishment of the Dawlat al-Iraq al-Islamiyah, "Islamic State of Iraq" (ISI) was announced.

[2] In April 2013, al-Baghdadi released an audio statement in which he announced that al-Nusra Front and the Islamic State of Iraq (ISI) were merging under the name "Islamic State of Iraq and Al-Sham" (ISIS).

[3] Sheikh Mohammad al-Fares of Tay tribe has established a militia as part of a national defence force that belongs to the Syrian regime.

[4] It is believed that Abu Mohammad al-Jawlani, the founder of JN, comes from this village.

5. The whole story of this uprising against ISIS can be found at the Global Post website: http://www.globalpost.com/dispatch/news/regions/middle-east/140811/who-are-the-tribesmen-standing-up-islamic-state-syria

References

Abdul-Ahad, G. (2012) Al-Qaida turns tide for rebels in battle for eastern Syria. *The Guardian*. Available from: http://www.theguardian.com/world/2012/jul/30/al-qaida-rebels-battle-syria [Accessed: 29,09, 2014].

Ahmed, A. (2013): *The Thistle and the Drone: How America's War on Terror Became a Global War on Tribal Islam.* Brookings Institution.

Ali, O. (2014): *Anbar Tribal Leader: Maliki Is 'More Dangerous' Than ISIS.* July 7 Available from: http://rudaw.net/english/interview/06072014 [Accessed:29,09, 2014].

Amnesty International. (2014a). *Gruesome evidence of ethnic cleansing in northern Iraq as Islamic State moves to wipe out minorities.* Available from: http://www.amnesty.org/en/news/gruesome-evidence-ethnic-cleansing-northern-iraq-islamic-state-moves-wipe-out-minorities-2014-0 [Accessed: 29,09,2014].

Dukhan, H. (2014) Tribes and Tribalism in the Syrian Uprising, *Syria Studies Journal*, Vol: 6, No: 02, pp. 1-27.

Gunaratna, R. & Nielsen, A. (2008) Al Qaeda in the Tribal Areas of Pakistan and Beyond, *International Centre for Political Violence and Terrorism Research, S. Rajaratnum School of International Studies*, Nanyang Technological University, Singapore. Available from: http://www.tandfonline.com/doi/pdf/10.1080/10576100802291568 [Accessed: 29,09, 2014].

Harling, P. (2014): What lies behind the "Islamic State" threat? *International Crisis Group*. 2 October. Available from: http://blog.crisisgroup.org/middle-east-north-africa/2014/10/02/what-lies-behind-the-islamic-state-threat/ [Accessed: 29,09, 2014].

Hassan. H. (2014): Isis: a portrait of the menace that is sweeping my homeland. *The Guardian*. [Online] August 16th. Available from: http://www.theguardian.com/world/2014/aug/16/isis-salafi-menace-jihadist-homeland-syria [Accessed: 29,09, 2014].

Hinnebusch,R. (2012) Syria: from 'Authoritarian Upgrading' to Revo-lution?" *Journal of International Affairs*. Vol: 88, No: 01, pp. 95-113.

Gerges, F. (2014). *Islamic State: Can its savagery be explained?*. [online] September 9th. Available from http://www.bbc.co.uk/news/world-middle-east-29123528. [Accessed: 13, 10, 2014].

Legal Reference. (2014). *Hiraba Legal Definition*. Available from: http://www.duhaime.org/LegalDictionary/H/Hiraba.aspx [Accessed: 29,09, 2014].

Ruthven, M. (2013):Terror: The Hidden Source. *The New York Review of Books*. [Online] October 24th. Available from: http://www.nybooks.com/articles/archives/2013/oct/24/terror-hidden-source/?pagination=false [Accessed: 29,09, 2014].

Salama, H. (2014) *How ISIS changed its game plan in Iraq*. [Online] July 14 Available from: http://www.al-monitor.com/pulse/politics/2014/07/syria-clans-isis.html##ixzz3Ej8sK1Q7 [Accessed: 29,09, 2014].

Salzman,P. (2008) *Culture and Conflict in the Middle East*. Prome-theus Books.

Sayigh, Y. (2014) ISIS: Global Islamic Caliphate or Islamic Mini-State in Iraq? *Carnegie Middle East*. [Online] July 24 Available from: http://carnegie-mec.org/2014/07/24/isis-global-islamic-caliphate-or-islamic-state-in-iraq [Accessed: 29,09, 2014].

Tabler, A. (2014): Reach Out to Arab Tribes in Eastern Syria. *The New York Times*. 23 September Available from: http://www.nytimes.com/roomfordebate/2014/09/23/strikes-on-isis-now-what/reach-out-to-arab-tribes-in-eastern-syria [Accessed: 29, 09, 2014].

أبو أمل الشمري , 2013: *Fourteen Tribes in Raqqa swear oath of loyalty to the Islamic State of Iraq and Levant*, [video online] Available at: http://www.youtube.com/watch?v=dz2XvvgEHWo [Accessed: 29,09, 2014].

6

Beyond Arms and Beards: Local Governance of ISIS in Syria

RANA KHALAF
UNIVERSITY OF SAINT ANDREWS, SCOTLAND (UK)

Introduction

The current situation in Syria presents complex governance dynamics. Its ongoing conflict is described as a mix of proxy regional and international wars, civil wars, and popular uprisings against authoritarianism. Between state-failure and war economy, this has rendered civil society in Syria a "conflict society" – an arena where multiple actors, both civil and uncivil, co-exist and compete. Thus, governance in Syria has come to be shaped by local and international interests, as well as by civil and uncivil actors (Khalaf, 2014).

Civil actors are a key component of a revived civil society in Syria. However, their agency, roles, and challenges are very different to those in peaceful democratic states. 'Local Coordination Committees' and local social movements have promoted civil disobedience against authoritarianism represented by the regime, sharia courts, armed groups, and other power perpetrators. These have delayed societal rifts along ethnic and sectarian lines. Others have worked on peace building and conflict resolution. Citizen journalists have raised awareness on human rights abuses. 'Local Councils' have alleviated human suffering by replacing the void created by the absent government in their provision of key public services. Local humanitarian organisations have provided food and shelter to affected populations. Other groups have been working on a variety of projects related to awareness creation, advocacy, development, and human rights, to the name but a few (Khalaf, et al., 2014; Khalaf, 2014). The challenges of this emerging civil society are many. Despite its goal of promoting a future inclusive democratic state, it has been diverted to respond to the conflict and its dire humanitarian needs first (Khalaf, et al., 2014). Meanwhile, it remains weak and fragmented and much limited. This is attributed to structural issues normally faced by civil societies under authoritarian rules, in addition to new limitations like its lack of security, resources, and support in the face of uncivil forces (Khalaf, 2014).

Uncivil actors in the Syrian conflict seem to be stronger than their civil counterparts. These include forces that do not share common causes and values for tolerance, justice, exclusion of violence, etc., which characterise the "civil" in civil society (Fischer, 2006). While uncivil actors have money, arms, and power, their networks extend beyond Syria to include nodes in other countries. These seem to be part of the agenda of new wars where the aim of violence is not so much directed against the 'enemy'; rather, it is to expand their networks to control territory through political and military means (Kaldor, 2003). Their technique is terror; violence against civilians is their deliberate war strategy (Kaldor, 2003). Soft power is also critical to this technique.

The Islamic State in Iraq and Greater Syria (ISIS) is one of these most powerful uncivil forces in Syria. ISIS is a predominantly jihadist group manipulating the country's instability to establish a caliphate – a single, transnational 'Islamic State' based on sharia (Zachary Laub, 2014). The group is said to have emerged in 2006 after the US-led invasion of Iraq. It appears to be a product of the Islamic State of Iraq, established by several Iraqi al-Qaeda-based or affiliated groups (Kfir, 2014). Whether ISIS has ever been affiliated with al-Qaeda beyond sharing work and resources is mired with controversy (Kfir, 2014). However, overt enmity between the two broke out in full in April 2014 (Zelin, 2014). Since then, ISIS has come to be even more extreme than al-Qaeda. At odds with al-Qaeda, ISIS seeks to expand its territorial control and establish a 'de facto' state in the borderlands of Syria and Iraq (Zachary Laub, 2014).

The brutality of ISIS and its ability to govern and expand has alarmed the international community that remains incapable of dealing with it effectively. Currently, a US-led anti-ISIS coalition of over 64 nations and groups continues to launch airstrikes in Syria and Iraq against it and other Islamist groups in the aim of weakening the group (National Post, 2014). However, according to local activists on the ground, this is only serving to expand the legitimacy of ISIS.[1] Some locals have since then moved their support to the group because their security and livelihoods have not been spared the striking. Rather, they are more in danger by both the coalition and the regime's shelling. This has promoted ISIS as the main group providing them with a form of security in contradiction to the international community. The latter is perceived as preaching human rights values that are never translated to any action to protect them, particularly as they continue to be targeted by the regime. This has expanded the acceptance of ISIS, and thus its governance ability. Consequently, without sufficient understanding of the governance dynamics of ISIS on the ground, efficacious policies will remain far-fetched. It is crucial to first understand how ISIS uses soft power, beyond its militarisation, to rule local populations in areas it controls.

The governance model during conflict

Studies on rebel groups in conflict suggest that "for a certain actor to govern, the governed must comply" (Keister & L. Slantchev, 2014). Coercion is a main factor in creating compliance, as physical and nutritional security may overwhelm other interests. However, civilians do have room to manoeuvre above a certain level. Considered as political actors, they have preferences and are capable of resisting and shaping their governor's governance tools.

The model developed in this study builds on three key governance tools that seem to facilitate the governability of local actors beyond coercion; these are effectiveness, legitimacy, and security. During conflict, locals perceive these differently from their international counterparts[2] – an issue that could explain the failure of international actors in dealing with conflict situations. At the local level during conflict, based on literature (Brikerhoff, 2005; Edwards, 2010; Mac Ginty, 2011; Roberts, 2011; Zoellick, 2008; Khalaf, 2014), this study defines these factors as follows:

Effectiveness: This is related to the regular and equitable provision of basic needs like electricity, water, food, jobs, etc. It also extends to cover more sustainable measures related to regenerating an economic cycle and livelihood opportunities.

Security: This is related to the capability to secure civilian lives. It involves managing security and order on the ground in a systematic, rather than ad hoc, manner. This is achieved via the creation, maintenance, and management of the relevant state functions of the police, judicial system, and armed groups. It also extends to defending infrastructure and sources of livelihood like power lines, pipelines, roads, and homes from looting and destruction.

Legitimacy: This refers to a social compact or complex set of beliefs and values (internal and external) governing state-society relations. It involves relationships, processes, and procedures. Part of these is also the capacity-related legitimacy, which relates to the provision of basic services and security measures in an accountable manner to citizens.

The governance dynamics of ISIS[3]

Coercion: ISIS has used and continues to use coercion, both directly and indirectly, to expand its control in Syria. In Al-Raqqa, for instance, ISIS has eliminated all local armed groups by either sending them out of the city or by forcing them to surrender to it via a *Bayaa*[4] (Khalaf, 2014). It also continues to ruthlessly punish individuals or groups opposing it. This is the fate of many civil society activists who have been detained, killed, or forced to leave the city (Khalaf, et al., 2014). ISIS's brutal and public punishment of its victims is an indirect form of coercion and warning of its ruthlessness to non-compliers. The ugly massacres it has carried against Al-Shaitat tribe that resisted it[5] were deliberate to market its coercive capability. These ensured that other tribes sought to pledge a Bayaa to ISIS or to reach negotiated deals with it. Meanwhile, the coercion mechanisms of ISIS extend to the forcible collection of taxes, seizure of houses, manipulation of livelihood sources, and control of resources such as oil, to name but a few examples. As such, non-compliance and resistance to ISIS is extremely risky and costly to the locals.

Nonetheless, while their choices are not free from coercion, it seems that in some cases civilians have unforcedly opted for compliance to ISIS, rather than to other powerful armed groups. In the recent fights in Dair Ezzor between ISIS and Al-Nusra Font (an Al-Qaeda-affiliated group), the locals, including the Free Syrian Army fighters, have chosen not to side with any of the two warring groups. As ISIS took over the city later on, it managed to win compliance from the locals. A key factor is not only its brutality, but also its better capability than its alternatives – be it other armed groups or 'local councils' – to provide effectiveness and security on the ground. In Dair Ezzor, before the invasion of ISIS, Al-Nusra Font has had strong governance over the city. However, Al-Nusra's ability to provide effectiveness in the provision of public goods and security on the ground has been crippling with corruption. In comparison to it, ISIS seemed to be the more legitimate and viable alternative of the two evils. As such, the non-coercive governance tools of ISIS shall be assessed below.

Effectiveness: Effectiveness in the provision of services generates more loyalty and compliance to those governing. This makes the rule of the governor more palatable. It causes less resentment for a slight increase in coercion. It may even generate voluntary support to them (Keister & L. Slantchev, 2014). ISIS is a typical example regarding these dynamics in the Syrian conflict. Across Syria's non-government controlled areas, ISIS is described as the most capable and efficient group in the provision of key social services to the locals. This is attributed to its well-structured institutions that are governed by a rigid set of rules and supported by massive resources.

With its sharia court, ISIS covers a wide array of state executive work in Al-Raqqa. This ranges from the provision of public goods and humanitarian aid, to the enforcement of its own form of law and justice system, and to the control of other aspects of the citizen's life. The latter includes housing policies, commercial laws, civil affairs, etc. ISIS's sharia court has offices and appointed personnel to a variety of these state functions. It even covers tribal affairs with its tribe's office to co-opt tribal members and preempt any regional efforts from organising tribes against it (Hassan, 2014b). Meanwhile, it has backed its sharia court with its 'Islamic Police' (Khalaf, 2014). This serves to ensure its policies and laws are effective and implemented. In support of this police is its strong state-like military, which is mainly composed of *muhajireen* or migrants. These have come from across the world to fight for the 'Islamic State'.

Meanwhile, as the provision of these services is costly, as a shadow state, ISIS has managed to expand its resources beyond its cross-border funding. The group depends on a well-planned war economy. It feeds off resources it has looted, and controls oil wells and flour-mills. Critically, it also collects income from taxes it imposes on locals (as Zakat), who, in their turn have complied. Many of them – especially the poor – have benefitted from the services provided by ISIS. This ranges from dispute management, to job placement, to food and shelter provision. In fact, locals in Al-Raqqa recount that, with the presence of ISIS, a form of a new economic cycle has been created in the city. For instance, as the only currency ISIS deals with is US dollars, currency exchange traders have mushroomed in the city center. Additionally, locals speak of food products in local shops like dates and honey that they have never seen before under the regime control. Thus, if civilians could ever choose between ISIS and an alternative, the weight of these services is a main factor they would consider. Meanwhile, ISIS coercion renders supporting alternatives to it more risky and costly.

Security: More than any other armed group, ISIS takes security on the ground seriously. In adhering to strict ideological rules, the group does not hesitate to use brutal force to ensure security maintenance. It first seeks to monopolise violence in the area it controls. In Al-Raqqa, it has managed to abolish all other local armed groups with its strong and highly trained jihadi fighters' military. It then became the only provider of security on the ground with its Islamic Police as its implementing arm and sharia court as the policy maker or 'state'. When not totally in control of an area, ISIS first appeals to locals exhausted by the conflict's chaos and insecurity, by focussing on eradicating groups behind looting. It then uses a mix of coercion and soft power to take full control of territory. This was the case in rural Dair Ezzor before ISIS expanded its control to take over Dair Ezzor city. It was also the case in Aleppo before ISIS was expelled from it by the more powerful and legitimate

Jaish Al Mujahideen group.

Meanwhile, as it continues to lack legitimacy on the ground due to its brutality and non-local identity, ISIS and its institutions are perceived as a protection from the chaos created by state failure and conflict. The locals, many of whom do not necessarily agree to its ideology and extremism, started using its court and police services, as these ensured their security. Additionally, the mere control of ISIS to a certain area is seen as a security measure from the random barrels of the regime. For instance, since the beginning of ISIS control of it, Al-Raqqa has rarely been targeted by the regime.

On the other end, due to its use of violence against the locals themselves, ISIS continues to be seen by many locals as personal security threat. On a small scale, it continues to be faced by non-violent and violent local resistance. Civil society actors have been fostering civil disobedience against it. Others have been targeting and killing its jihadi members at night, when entering neighbourhoods heavily populated by locals. ISIS is not blind to the fact that its brutality has ensured it is affecting the acceptance of locals to it (Khalaf, 2014). To solve this issue, it has focused on its capacity to gain legitimacy. ISIS has been promoting a more palatable form of citizenship than that of corrupt leaders and regimes in Syria and Iraq. Once citizens of its 'Islamic State' abide by its rules, locals are promised security – physical, economic, social, and religious (Kfir, 2014). This citizenship is palatable because ISIS has indeed managed to provide immediate physical security. Unlike other rebel groups, it has at least provided the promise of eventual economic security (Kfir, 2014).

Legitimacy: Beyond its capacity-related legitimacy, ISIS understands that its brutal processes and procedures against the locals continue to limit its legitimacy. This is especially the case as its extremist beliefs and values are far from the average Sunni local in Syria. Even so, ISIS does not intend to change its ways or its strict ideology. Rather, it seeks to increase its legitimacy by either co-opting the locals by building relationships with them, or by changing their ideology towards it.

With regards to its relationship-building efforts, as areas it controls are mainly tribal, ISIS pays particular focus on tribal affairs. To manipulate them with a divide-and-rule tactic, it seems to build on its long experience in operating amongst tribes. Hassan (2014) explains this process: understanding local social and tribal rivalry and hostility to each other, ISIS has been successful in pitting tribes and members of a tribe against each other. First, it has secretly sought the loyalty of and alliance with influential tribal leaders. With these then came pledges that include sharing financial revenues for the promotion of tribal figures to future influential positions at the expense of existing leaders. Thus, by empowering tribes to govern their own state of affairs in allegiance to it, ISIS seems to be indirectly managing some of them. On an analysis of *Dabiq*, ISIS's online magazine, Gambhir (2014) summarizes that, as the authority of ISIS continued to expand, tribes themselves started seeking to allege a "Bayaa" to it. In doing so, tribes benefit from ISIS's aid and non-coercion in return for complying with it. Militarily, this is by providing financial aid, fighters, and weapons to ISIS. Politically, this is via tax contribution (zakat) (Gambhir, 2014). In this manner, ISIS has ensured it reaps maximum benefit from its relationship with the tribes while building a difficult-to-break authority over them.

Regarding its ideological infiltration efforts, ISIS has sought to persuade the locals into its ideology. Its leaders seem to understand the core of the theory of Keister and Slantchev (2014), which suggests that, while they may not be able to articulate it, civilians do have ideological preferences – over their relationship with the state, religion, land reform, etc. The ideological distance between those governing and the preferences of these citizens, rather than the ideology itself, is key in governability. It makes civilians sceptical about the intentions of those governing, and thus less cooperative with them. This is despite the effectiveness of those governing in the provision of services and security.

To minimise this ideological distance, ISIS has been working on diverting local ideology towards its own by investing heavily in justifying its religious ideology and rival organisations. ISIS continues to produce religious, military, and political arguments to market the correctness and ultimate solidity and victory of its Islamic State (Gambhir, 2014). It backs these by its political institutions and by a sound media strategy. The most evident example of this is the ISIS online magazine *Dabiq*. *Dabiq* eloquently articulates the vision of ISIS, justifies its authority, forwards its arguments, and highlights its progress to its followers (Gambhir, 2014). Building on religious justification, it aims to build the religious legitimacy of ISIS and its 'Islamic State', while encouraging Muslims to emigrate there (Gambhir, 2014). Albeit extreme, the discourse of this 'Islamic State' may increasingly appeal to those whom world human rights, democracy, and other ideological discourses have failed them as they continue to face death, torture, and losses at all levels by predatory nation-states.

Policy implications

Theoretically, Keister and Stantchev (2014) suggest that foreign sponsors and domestic counterinsurgency efforts may challenge rebel governance dynamics by changing their relative costs of coercion and service provision. In pursuing these changes, the model highlights that international policymakers and donors are at a dilemma. While military assistance may be critical to press the government, this may increase human rights violations and radicalise rebels, as it lowers the price of coercion. Conversely, while much needed, humanitarian aid might enable rebels to take advantage of more-affordable service provision, thus boasting their governance, even if radical. Accordingly, the model recommends that donors 'tame' rebels by inducing them to relatively more moderate ideologies and actions through the form and amount of aid they offer.

Seemingly, many donors in Syria have adhered to this recommendation. The implications of increased aid-related radicalisation are real and need not be ignored. However, what the model misses is that when moderate forces (albeit difficult to define) lose military and service support, governance moves to other, better-resourced extreme forces like ISIS. Thus, the implications of holding resources from other viable alternatives to radical groups are also critical. To balance the power dynamics, support can also come in other forms than what is military or humanitarian, and to other local actors, like civil society actors, who could better hold rebels accountable. Without sufficient support, civil society will continue to face resource, financial, and security limitations. Thus, to ensure aid effectiveness, local grassroots civil society on the ground needs to be supported. Dair Ezzor provides a good illustration of this shortcoming of the international approach in dealing with governance dynamics in Syria. Right upon the overtake of Dair Ezzor by ISIS, many donors have held back their support to local civil society actors and 'local councils' out of fear of 'funding terrorism' if resources become redirected to ISIS. However, these policies are limiting, on the other hand, the capacity of other alternatives to ISIS to provide public goods effectively and, thus, to challenge ISIS's governance.

Another critical governance aspect the international community is missing on in Syria is security. International actors seem to be more involved in their own security from ISIS's expansion and terrorist influx to their countries, rather than the security of the locals in Syria (Khalaf, 2014). At a greater level, and on a longer period to that faced by ISIS, the security of Syrian civilians on the ground has been and continues to be targeted by the regime's random shelling. However, the international community has opted for only an anti-ISIS coalition that yet again ignores the regime. Such international actions have come to be seen by the locals as increasing the coercive capability of the regime (Ian & Mona, 2014). This is triggering a local reaction in support of ISIS (Hassan, 2014), which, albeit brutal, is at least working on the provision of security on the ground.

On a more positive note, it seems one governance factor ISIS has not yet well mastered is legitimacy. International policy can serve to further weaken the legitimacy of ISIS by supporting local alternatives to it that are civil and inclusive. Capacity-related legitimacy may be promoted by supporting effective service delivery via local councils and civil society simultaneously. It could be furthered with re-constituting security on the ground by primarily protecting the locals and their institutions from the random shelling of the regime. Meanwhile, although as far-fetched a dream as that of global civil society, the credibility of human rights values in the face of extremism needs to be reconstructed and applied impartially against power perpetrators ranging from the regime to ISIS to international actors who have supported human rights violations. Following these procedures, the locals will have more motivation and may face less risk and costs in rising against ISIS. Without understanding and investing in these local dynamics alongside the international dynamics sustainably, ISIS, anti-ISIS plans are doomed to fail.

Notes

1. See also (Ian & Mona , 2014) and (Hassan, 2014a).
2. For further explanation on how international actors perceive governance in Syria, see (Khalaf, Governance without Government in Syria: Civil Society and State-Building during Conflict, 2014).
3. This section relies on primary data from interviews with local civil activists unless otherwise stated.
4. A form of Islamic social contract in which the ruled express loyalty to the ruler (Kaldor, 2003).
5. See (The Washington Post, 2014).

References

Brikerhoff, D., 2005. Rebuilding Governance in Failed States and Post-Conflict Societies: Core Concepts and Cross-Cutting Themes. *Public Administration and Development*, Volume 25, pp. 3-15.

Edwards, L., 2010. State-building in Afghanistan: A Case Showing the Limits?. *International Review of the Red Cross*, 92(880), pp. 967-991.

Fischer, M., 2006. *Civil Society in Conflict Transformation: Ambivalence, Potentials and Challenges,* Berghof: Berghof Research Center for Constructive Conflict Management.

Gambhir, H. K., 2014. *Backgrounder - Dabiq: The Strategic Messaging of the Islamic State,* s.l.: Institute for the Study of War.

Hassan, H., 2014. *Isis Exploits Tribal Fault Lines to Control its Territory.* [Online] Available at: http://www.theguardian.com/world/2014/oct/26/isis-exploits-tribal-fault-lines-to-control-its-territory-jihadi [Accessed 29 10 2014].

Hassan, H., 2014. *What the Isis Jihadis Lose in Strength from the Air Strikes They May Gain in Legitimacy.* [Online] Available at: http://www.theguardian.com/commentisfree/2014/sep/28/what-isis-loses-strength-air-strikes-gain-legitimacy [Accessed 17 10 2014].

Ian, B. & Mona, M., 2014. *Coalition Air Strikes Against Isis Aid Bashar Al-Assad, Syrian Rebels Claim.* [Online] Available at: http://www.theguardian.com/world/2014/oct/09/syria-isis-bashar-al-assad-coalition-air-strikes [Accessed 15 10 2014].

Kaldor, M., 2003. *Global Civil Society: An Answer to War.* Cambridge: Polity Press.

Keister, . J. & L. Slantchev, . B., 2014. *Statebreakers to Statemakers:Strategies of Rebel Governance.* [Online] Available at: http://slantchev.ucsd.edu/wp/pdf/RebelGovern-W079.pdf [Accessed 27 10 2014].

Kfir, I., 2014. *Social Identity Group and Human (In)Security: The Case of Islamic State in Iraq and the Levant (ISIS),* Syracuse: Institute for National Security & Counterterrorism (INSCT).

Khalaf, R., 2014. *Governance without Government in Syria: Civil Society and State-Building during Conflict*, St Andrews: Syria Studies Journal (Forthcoming).

Khalaf, R., Ramadan, O. & Stollies, F., 2014. *Activism in Difficult Times: Civil Society in Syria (2011-2014)*, Beirut: Friedrich-Ebert-Stiftung (Forthcoming).

Mac Ginty, R., 2011. *International Peacebuilding and Local Resistance: Hybrid Forms of Peace.* Hampshire: Palgrave Macmillan.

National Post, 2014. Anti-ISIS Coalition Has Mobilized up to 62 Nations and Groups. [online] Available at: http://news.nationalpost.com/2014/09/26/mobilizing-the-world-up-to-62-nations-and-groups-have-joined-coalition-against-isis/ [Accessed 27 10 2014].

Roberts, D., 2011. *Liberal Peacebuilding and Global Governance: Beyond the Metropolis.* New York: Routeledge Studies in Peace and Conflict Resolution.

The Washington Post, 2014. *Syria Tribal Revolt against Islamic State Ignored, Fueling Resentment.* [Online] Available at: http://www.washingtonpost.com/world/syria-tribal-revolt-against-islamic-state-ignored-fueling-resentment/2014/10/20/25401beb-8de8-49f2-8e64-c1cfbee45232_story.html [Accessed 01 11 2014].

Zachary Laub, 2014. *Backgrounders: Islamic State in Iraq and Syria.* [Online] Available at: http://www.cfr.org/iraq/islamic-state-iraq-syria/p14811 [Accessed 25 10 2014].

Zelin, A. Y., 2014. The War between ISIS and al-Qaeda for Supremacy of the Global Jihadist Movement. *Research Notes*, 20 06, Volume 20, pp. 1-11.

Zoellick, R., 2008. Fragile States: Securing Development. *Survival: Global Politics and Strategy,* 50(6), pp. 67-84.

7

The Islamic State and its Viability

MOHAMMED NURUZZAMAN
GULF UNIVERSITY FOR SCIENCE AND TECHNOLOGY, KUWAIT

The rise of the Islamic State (IS), previously called the ISIS (Islamic State of Iraq and al-Sham) or the ISIL (Islamic State in Iraq and the Levant), is more than an explosive event in the traditionally volatile Middle East region. Proclaimed on 29 June 2014, the IS, which captured and now controls huge swathes of territories straddling northwestern Iraq and eastern Syria, is in a state of war against the whole world. The self-styled caliph of the IS, Abu Bakr al-Baghdadi, made his first official speech the same day. He divided the whole world into two camps – 'the camp of Islam and faith, and the camp of *kufr* (disbelief) and hypocrisy'.[1] He put the Muslims and the mujahidin in the first camp; the Jews, the crusaders, and their allies (meaning America's Arab allies), and the rest of the nations (including Shiite apostates in Iran and elsewhere) fill the second camp.

This new division of the world strictly on religious lines, coupled with IS's lightning military offensives and rapid victories over the US-trained and equipped Iraqi defense forces, soon rang alarm bells of serious proportions in Tehran, Riyadh, and Washington, unleashing diplomatic realignments across the region and coordinated military actions to halt advances by IS militants. Erstwhile bitter rivals Iran and Saudi Arabia are closing their ranks to face the common IS threat (Reuters, 2014); Iran and the US are engaged in 'give and take' talks over the nuclear issue to devise a common strategy to stop the IS (CNBC, 2014a); and President Obama has forged a military coalition, consisting of Gulf Arab allies and some European states, to 'degrade and destroy' the IS (*The Wall Street Journal*, 2014a).

Surprisingly, the IS, despite mounting military pressures and financial sanctions (*The Huffington Post,* 2014a), continues to launch relentless military offensives to capture more urban centres and territories, both in Iraq and Syria. But can it survive the US-led air strikes and Iran-supported counter-attacks (Branen, 2014) by the Iraqi and Syrian armies? This article cross-checks the military, economic, and political viability of the IS in long-term perspectives. It concludes that the IS is a reality and it is here to stay, whether we like it or not. Moreover, the IS looks to have set for gradual expansion of its territorial boundaries to ultimately redraw the political map of the Middle East.

What explains the rise of the IS?

Academics and journalists alike take the position that the former Nouri al-Maliki government was primarily culpable for the rise of the IS, while the sectarianism-driven civil war in Syria fed into the process (Phillips, 2014; Kayaoğlu, 2014). That the al-Maliki government was divisive, did not pursue the right policies to integrate the minority Sunnis in his government, and failed to create a sense of Iraqi national identity are true. But they fall short of accounting for the violent outbreak of armed conflict and capture of territories by the IS. Discriminatory socio-economic and political policies based on sectarian paranoia are nothing new in Iraq or, for that matter, in other Arab states in the Gulf (Nasr, 2007). The late Saddam Hussein's anti-Shiites and anti-Kurds policies galvanised resistance to his regime, but not on such a dangerous scale as we currently see in Iraq. The Sunni-dominated regimes in Bahrain and Saudi Arabia are also known for their anti-Shiite policies, but there is no IS-type violence brewing up there.

The Syrian civil war drew groups of so-called moderate and al-Qaeda fighters with political and financial backings from regional and global actors to topple President Bashar al-Assad. It definitely created the ripe situations for the jihadists to train new recruits and master fighting skills, but a sudden turn to establish an Islamic caliphate by the IS, an al-Qaeda offshoot, taking advantage of a bloody civil war sounds somewhat anachronistic. In fact, there are other deeply rooted factors behind the emergence of the IS.

The rise of the IS boils down to the long lineage of Islamic movements for the revival of Muslim power and glory, lost after the disintegration of the Ottoman Empire following World War One and the formal abolition of the Islamic Caliphate in 1924. The Islamists see historical conspiracies and secret dealings by the European powers, such as the Sykes-Picot Agreement of May 1916 and the Balfour Declaration of November 1917, to dominate and keep the Muslims under control. As for the actual decline of Muslim power, many scholars have identified deviation from *Sharia* (Quranic laws) as the principal reason, and a return to *Sharia*, they argue, is the only way to revive the glorious past, restore global leadership, and lead the world. This is the basic premise of operations by movements like the Muslim Brotherhood in the Arab world, Jamaat-e-Islami in South Asia, and al-Qaeda on a global scale (Akberzade, 2012). Abu Bakr al-Baghdadi's IS, like its parent organisation al-Qaeda, is also squarely premised on the same ground – a return to Sharia and the re-establishment of Islam as a global force. The mayhem in Iraq following the 2003 US invasion, the internecine Shiite-Sunni sectarian war, the al-Maliki government's anti-Sunni policies, and the Syrian civil war played contributory roles behind what is now the IS.

In his first speech at the Grand Mosque in Mosul soon after the proclamation of the IS, al-Baghdadi emphasised the need for establishing the Sharia and specifically said, "The establishment of a caliphate is an obligation. The religion cannot be in place unless the *Sharia* is established" (al-Jazeera, 2014a). And his division of the world, already mentioned in the introductory section, into the two opposing camps of Muslims and non-Muslims, implied a fight between the two camps, which is presumably being fought in Iraq and Syria currently. He winded up his speech with a clarion call to all Muslims to unite under the IS flag. The call for Muslim unity to uphold the IS has been mostly greeted with condemnations worldwide, barrages of air strikes by the US and allies, and ground military actions to finish off al-Baghdadi's IS.

Cross-checking the IS's viability

The IS's rapid territorial gains in Iraq have brought it an unprecedented opportunity to declare itself a state. It is not, however, a state as it is understood in Western political parlance – a state with the four basic elements of territory, population, government, and sovereignty. The Westphalian system of states, which dates back to 1648, survives on the principles of autonomy and sovereignty for a people with a fixed territory. The IS, based on the idea of *khilafah* (Islamic political system), does not fit this category. Under the *khilafah*, all Muslims are members of a single community of believers called *ummah*, share a common feeling of solidarity called *assabiya*, and are ruled by a single caliph. The IS currently lacks all these qualities, though it aspires to establish a *khilafah* eventually.

The first issue of *Dabiq*, IS's official mouthpiece, mentioned above, carries the cover story 'The Return of Khilafah' and declares that "The time has come for the Ummah of Muhammad (sallallahu 'alayhi wa sallam) to wake up from its sleep, remove the garments of dishonour, and shake off the dust of humiliation and disgrace, for the era of lamenting and moaning has gone, and the dawn of honour has emerged anew" (p. 7). This call resonates well with the feelings and aspirations of many young Muslims across the world who are flocking to join the IS fighting group. This is, however, the second time that a *khilafah* has been declared after the demolition of the Ottoman Empire. In 1924, Sherif Hussein bin Ali of Mecca, a descendent of Prophet Muhammad (peace be upon him), proclaimed himself the caliph of all Muslims. He was later defeated by King Abdulaziz Al-Saud who, after conquering most of the Arabian Peninsula, founded the Kingdom of Saudi Arabia in 1932.

Al-Baghdadi's IS may be viewed as a de facto state, at best, with territorial control from Syria's al-Raqqah province, to Mosul in northern Iraq, to Fallujah and Abu Ghraib in central Iraq – an area roughly equal to the size of Belgium; some eight million people live in IS territory (BBC, 2014a), it has a small army of up to 31,000 troops (BBC, 2014b), and provides a loose form of governance. There is no international recognition for the IS, nor has the IS sought such recognition. Basically, the IS remains an extra-legal reality on the ground, with question marks on its future political, military, and economic survival.

Political viability

The biggest crisis the IS faces is the crisis of political legitimacy. Caliph al-Baghdadi's call on Muslims to join and support the IS has drawn fire from multiple jihadist organisations. Previously, al-Qaeda chief Ayman al-Zawahiri condemned the IS's brutal war tactics and its war on other rebel groups in Syria. Al-Zawahiri also formally disavowed IS in February this year. But he has neither publicly condemned nor stood by the declaration of Khilafah by al-Baghdadi. The Islamic Front, a loose alliance of rebel groups seeking to overthrow the Bashar Al-Assad government and establish Islamic rule in Syria, has rejected the declaration, branding it as divisive and lacking any legitimacy (Al Jazeera, 2014b). At the same time, several al-Qaeda allies have broken ranks and declared allegiance to the IS. A section of the AQIM (Al-Qaeda in the Arabian Peninsula) led by the cleric Mamoun Hatem has openly pledged loyalty to the IS; the Afghan jihadi group Hezb-e-Islami was the next to support the IS; Ansar Bayt al-Maqdis, an Egyptian jihadi group, maintains ties with the IS; Libyan jihadists grouped under the banner of Ansar al-Sharia in Libya are loyal to the IS (Berger, 2014). So increasingly the IS is expanding its network of allies and supporters, posing a direct challenge to al-Qaeda and al-Zawahiri's leadership.

Outside the mainstream jihadi organisations, many Sunni religious scholars have denounced the IS. Qatar-based Egyptian Sunni leader Yusuf al-Qaradawi views the declaration of *khilafah* as a violation of Islamic law. He opined that the declaration was a misstep aimed to damage the cause of the

Sunnis in Iraq and Syria. The Jordanian Salafi leader Abu Muhammad al-Maqdisi labeled the IS group as 'deviant', a group out to damage the image of Islam (Al Jazeera, 2014c). Muslim religious leaders and scholars from different world regions, including the grand mufti of Egypt, Sheikh Shawqi Allam, and the mufti of Jerusalem and All of Palestine, Sheikh Muhammad Ahmad Hussein, issued an open letter to al-Baghdadi in late September and unequivocally denounced the IS as "un-Islamic" (*The Huffington Post*, 2014b).

The political legitimacy crisis put aside, at the practical level, there is a dearth of information on the political structures and processes of the IS; there hardly exists any information on the administrative management and political institutions building by the IS to run state affairs. Even though the IS is not a state in the Westphalian sense, it cannot avoid building capacities in the areas of taxation, administration of justice, adjudication of disputes, and the creation of security provisions for the eight million people who live on its territory, willingly or under force. IS's official publication *Dabiq* carries no comprehensive stories on these important issues, though there are sporadic references to administrative and security issues at the local tribal council level. Issue number one of *Dabiq* (p. 13), after referring to a meeting with tribal representatives in Halab region in Syria, reports the benefits and services the IS provides to its people.[2] These include the return of property rights to their legal owners, spending money to provide people with required services, promotion of security for people under IS's control, ensuring food security for the people, a strict check on crimes, and the promotion of ties between the IS and its people.

Apparently the IS is active at the grass-roots, community level to look after the needs and services of people under its authority, but more complex issues of monetary management, justice system, administrative set-up, state institutions building, etc. seem to remain unaddressed. Lack of state capacity building in all these areas means a serious challenge to the political viability of the IS.

Military viability

If political viability of the IS is in obscurity, its military survival is more or less secure. With some 30,000 battle-hardened, ruthless fighters and huge quantities of captured sophisticated weapons from the Iraqi and Syrian armies, the IS is so far proving itself militarily unbeatable. The tightening grip on Kobane, a Kurdish town on the Syria-Turkey border, countless air strikes to blunt IS fighters' advance notwithstanding, attests to this point. In the Iraqi province of Anbar, the IS fighters are reported to have scored a number of military victories between 1-7 October. A blog post by the Institute for the

Study of War reports that most of the territory from Qaim on the Syrian border to Abu Ghraib, a town close to Baghdad International Airport, is now controlled by the IS fighters. This critical gain poses serious threats to Iraqi army supply lines and reinforcements in Anbar (Squires and Petrocine, 2014).

Behind the audacious military advances by the IS, there are two factors in play – the jihadi zeal of the IS fighters, and a defective US strategy to confront the IS. The IS fighters are fearless, driven, according to their belief, by a religious cause to fight and defeat the infidels, the enemies of Islam. They are ready to fight and die until the IS becomes a reality globally. The second issue of their magazine *Dabiq* refers to the story of the ark of Noah, which he, under God's instructions, made to avoid the cataclysmic flood that swiped away the disbelievers. Drawing on this story, the IS has developed its operational motto: "It's either the Islamic State or the flood". An extra boost for IS fighters' morale comes from unbelievable military successes of the Muslim armies against the Persian and Byzantine empires in the early period of Islam, to which the IS-controlled al-Hayat Media Center and website often refer to. In the Battle of Qadisiyyah, fought in 636, the Arab army of 30,000 men forced a crushing defeat on the Persian army of 200,000 fighters. Such stories well feed into the indomitable courage of the IS fighters to face their enemies.

The spirit of the IS fighters outmatches that of the Iraqi and Syrian armies and their supporters – Iran and the US-led coalition. While Iran is deeply involved in the fight against the IS, President Obama's two-pronged strategy of air operations and arming IS's opponents, according to critics, will fail to yield the desired results. In his speech to the American nation on 10 September 2014, Obama identified the IS as a threat to the broader Middle East region and loosely connected the threat to American security. "If left unchecked, these terrorists could pose a growing threat beyond that region – including to the United States", he emphasised.[3]

The critical question is how realistic is the president's air campaign strategy against the IS. Obama may have been encouraged by the successes of NATO's 78-day strategic air campaign against the Serbian forces in the 1999 Kosovo War, or the long air operations to topple the Muammar Gaddafi government in 2011, but the IS is a different enemy in terms of fighting skills, battlefield brutality, and possession of modern weaponry. The IS militants have also seen the inability of the Israeli air force to destroy Hamas military personnel and capacities in the latest war on Gaza fought during last July and August. Israel's air operations against Hamas, codenamed 'Operation Protective Edge', have clearly failed to destroy Hamas military might in Gaza, an area 41 miles long and eight miles wide (Haas, 2014). Contrarily, after the war, Hamas has emerged more popular, and may emerge more powerful in future.

Former and current US defence and security officials have cast doubt about the success of Obama's anti-IS strategy. Robert Gates, former Secretary of Defence, said on ABC's *This Week* in mid-September that the president's goal to "degrade and destroy" the IS was a "very ambitious goal". "A realistic objective", he believes, is "to try and push them out of Iraq and deny them a permanent foothold some place" (Press TV, 2014a). The poor performance of airstrikes on IS fighters and military facilities also led Obama to admit that the US intelligence officials underestimated the IS and overestimated the capacity of the Iraqi defence forces to fend off the IS militants (Fox News, 2014). Additionally, Obama's plan to train and equip the moderate Syrian forces to combat the IS forces has so far been a non-starter. Back in early September, the AFP (2014) circulated a story that the IS had signed a 'non-aggression' pact with moderate and Islamist rebels not to attack each other until the fall of the Bashar Al-Assad government. It simply undercut the success potential of Obama's anti-IS strategy further.

In a realistic analysis, the critical factors that eat into the success of Obama's current anti-IS strategy include the president's unwillingness to commit US ground troops required to drive out and regain territories from IS fighters, the reluctance of allies to offer boots on the ground to stave off the IS military onslaught, and the capacity of the IS to turn odd situations to its favour. In the absence of a credible military strategy involving ground and air operations, the IS is most likely to broaden its military march and score more victories.

Economic viability

Economically, the IS seems to be placed in a comfortable zone. It is believed to control assets worth US $2 billion and has sizeable cash reserves primarily accumulating from oil revenues in Iraq and Syria (CNBC, 2014b). Currently, the IS controls eight oil and gas fields in eastern Syria that produce between 300,000 and 700,000 barrels of oil a day. The IS sells heavy oil at a much reduced rate of $26 to $35 a barrel to Iraqi, Lebanese, and Turkish businessmen (*The Wall Street Journal*, 2014b). In the Iraqi territories under IS control, the picture is more the same. The June blitzkrieg ended up with the acquisition of seven Iraqi oil fields, with a production capacity of 80,000 barrels of oil a day, by the IS. The potential daily income from these oil fields amounts to $8.4 million a day. Furthermore, the IS controls government food silos in northern and northwestern Iraq – the wheat producing belt of the country (Press TV, 2014b).

The implications are clear. The IS has a sustainable economy at its disposal to mitigate the pressures of global economic sanctions. That is likely to give it an opportunity fund its continuous military operations and to win the support of its eight million Iraqis and Syrians by not taxing them too much. The IS may even dispense quality social and security services to the people to promote its image and neutralise internal opposition or rebellion. The provision of food security, the IS enjoys, further promises it a tranquil social order, at least for the time being.

Conclusion

The discussion and analysis in this short article underscore three important points: 1) The IS is an outcome of complex factors ranging from pan-Islamic political movements to revive the *khilafah* to contemporary domestic and international policies in Iraq and the Middle East. 2) In the past few months, the IS has emerged strong; it is a reality with its own territories carved out of Iraq and Syria. The failure of the US-led coalition and regional states to seriously weaken the IS may put more territories under its control. 3) The IS operates from a strong military and economic base that apparently guarantees its survival on a long-term basis, though it has yet to deal with challenges to its political viability. The long-term survival of the IS means a new Middle East, a Middle East with redrawn state boundaries.

Notes

[1] See the first issue of Dabiq, the official magazine of the IS, published in the Arabic month of Ramadan, 1435(H), at: https://ia902500.us.archive.org/24/items/dbq01_desktop_en dbq01_desktop_en.pdf; accessed: 5 October 2014.
[2] See Dabiq, Issue No. 2, accessed at: https://azelin.files.wordpress.com/2014/07/islamic-state-e2809cdc481biq-magazine-2e280b3.pdf, 4 October 2014.
[3] Transcript of President Obama's speech can be accessed at: http://www.npr.org/2014/09/10/347515100/transcript-president-obama-on-how-u-s-will-address-islamic-state, 10 September 2014.

References

AFP (2014), "*Syria rebels, IS in 'non-aggression' pact near Damuscus*", 12 September, accessed at: http://www.globalpost.com/dispatch/news/afp/140912/syria-rebels-non-aggression-pact-near-damascus, 5 October 2014.

Akberzade, S. (ed.) (2012), *Routledge Handbook of Political Islam* (London: Taylor and Francis).

Al Jazeera (2014a), *"Islamic State's 'caliph' lauds Iraq rebellion"*, 6 July, accessed at: http://www.aljazeera.com/news/middleeast/2014/07/islamic-state-caliph-lauds-iraq-rebellion-20147512574517772.html, 20 September 2014.

Al Jazeera (2014b), *"Baghdadi's vision of a new caliphate"*, 1 July, accessed at: http://www.aljazeera.com/news/middleeast/2014/07/baghdadi-vision-new-caliphate-20147184858247981.html, 2 October 2014.

Al Jazeera (2014c), *"Islamic State's 'caliph' lauds Iraq rebellion"* (link referred to above).

BBC News (2014a), *"What is Islamic State?"*, 26 September, accessed at: http://www.bbc.com/news/world-middle-east-29052144, 3 October 2014.

BBC News (2014b), *"Islamic State fighter estimate triples – CIA"*, 12 September, accessed at: http://www.bbc.com/news/world-middle-east-29169914, 3 October 2014.

Berger, J. M. (2014), "The Islamic State vs. al-Qaeda", *Foreign Policy*, 2 September, accessed at:http://www.foreignpolicy.com/articles/2014/09/02/islamic_state_vs_al_qaeda_next_jihadi_super_power, 7 September 2014.

Brannen, K. (2014), "Tehran's Boots on the Ground", *Foreign Policy*, 10 September, accessed at: http://complex.foreignpolicy.com/posts/2014/09/10/tehrans_boots_on_the_ground_iraq_syria_islamic_state_isis_iran, 11 September 2014.

CNBC (2014a), *"Iran seeks give and take on militants, nuclear program"*, 21 September 2014, accessed at: http://www.cnbc.com/id/102019065, 7 October 2014.

CNBC (2014b), *"How ISIS managed to acquire $2B in assets"*, 16 June, accessed at: http://www.cnbc.com/id/101761986#., 6 October 2014.

Fox News (2014), *"Obama says US 'underestimated' rise of ISIS, admits 'contradictory' Syria policy'*, 29 September, accessed at: http://www.foxnews.com/politics/2014/09/29/us-misjudged-iraqi-army-isis-threat-obama-says/, 5 October 2014.

Haas, M. C. (2014), "Israel's Operation Protective Edge: Showcase for the Limits of Precision Strike?", *The National Interest*, 01 August, accessed at: http://nationalinterest.org/feature/israel%E2%80%99s-operation-protective-edge-showcase-the-limits-10997, 2 October 2014.

Kayaoğlu, B. (2014), "Five Axioms to Remember about ISIS and Iraq", *The National Interest*, 25 June, accessed at: http://nationalinterest.org/feature/five-axioms-remember-about-isis-iraq-10747, 27 September 2014.

Nasr, V. (2007), *The Shia Revival: How Conflicts within Islam will Shape the Future* (New York: W.W. Norton & Company; Reprint Edition).

Phillips, A. (2014), "The Islamic State's challenge to international order", *Australian Journal of International Affairs*, Vol. 68, No. 5, pp. 495-498.

Press TV (2014a), *"Gates: Obama's ISIL plan not realistic"*, 21 September, accessed at: http://www.presstv.com/detail/2014/09/21/379544/gates-obamas-isil-plan-not-realistic/, 5 October 2014.

Press TV (2014b), *"There is no parallel between ISIL and Viet Kong: Don DeBar"*, 21 September, accessed at: http://www.presstv.ir/detail/2014/09/21/379452/isil-is-construct-of-cia-us-journalist/, 7 October 2014.

Reuters (2014), *"Minds focused by IS, Saudis and Iranians think of making up"*, 22 September 2014, accessed at: http://news.yahoo.com/iran-foreign-minister-hails-chapter-saudi-ties-irna-084551733.html, 5 October 2014.

Squires L. and Petrocine, N. (2014), *"ISIS Advances in Anbar (September 1 – October 7)*, 8 October, accessed at: http://iswiraq.blogspot.com/2014/10/isis-advances-in-anbar-september-1.html?utm_source=ISIS+Advances+in+Anbar+%28September+1-October+7%2C+2014%29&utm_campaign=ISW+New+Iraq+update&utm_medium=email

The Huffington Post (2014a) "The UN Strikes Back at ISIL's Black Economy", 23 August 2014, accessed at: http://www.huffingtonpost.com/luay-al-khatteeb/the-un-strikes-back-at-isil_b_5702240.html, 24 August 2014.

The Huffington Post (2014b), "Muslim Scholars Release Open Letter to Islamic State Meticulously Blasting Its Ideology", 24 September, accessed at: http://www.huffingtonpost.com/2014/09/24/muslim-scholars-islamic-state_n_5878038.html, 26 September 2014.

The Wall Street Journal (2014a), "U.S. Aims to 'Degrade and Destroy' Militants", 3 September, accessed at: http://online.wsj.com/articles/obama-says-us-aims-to-shrink-islamic-states-sphere-of-influence-1409743189, 6 October 2014.

The Wall Street Journal (2014b), "Islamic State Economy Runs on Extortion, Oil Piracy in Syria, Iraq", 28 August, accessed at: http://online.wsj.com/articles/islamic-state-fills-coffers-from-illicit-economy-in-syria-iraq-1409175458, 10 September 2014.

8

What is Islamic Democracy? The Three Cs of Islamic Governance

M. A. MUQTEDAR KHAN
UNIVERSITY OF DELAWARE, USA

What is Islamic Democracy? Is it a secular democracy in which Islamic leaning parties come to power and Islamic identity influences policy choices, as in Turkey? Or is it, like Iran, a theo-democracy in which Islam and Islamic values are constitutionally privileged and mandated, and where elections serve merely to elect the executive while the legislative function remains subordinate to Islamic law – The divine *Sharia*?

Islamists for decades have been striving to bring Islamic values to bear on the politics of their societies. There are many shades of Islamists, and they are advancing many different political models that integrate religious values, religious identity, and politics. Some are seeking to establish Islamic states in Muslim majority states (Egypt, Tunisia, Pakistan), some are seeking to establish a global Caliphate (Syria and Iraq), and others are fighting to break away from non-Muslim States (Kashmir and Palestine). The underlying assumption of all these political movements is that Islamic sources postulate a blueprint for governance, and includes the establishment of an Islamic state.

Since the collapse of the Muslim Brotherhood's government in Egypt in 2013, Islamists by and large have assumed the mantle of democracy and now call for democratisation and oppose authoritarianism. The calls to establish Islamic States and impose Islamic laws are limited to fringe, but armed, violent and increasingly brutal militias such as ISIS (Islamic state in Iraq and

Syria) and the TTP (Tehrik-e-Taliban Pakistan), the Taliban movement in Pakistan. ISIS, which now controls a vast swath of area in Syria and Iraq, has even declared the establishment of the caliphate and named their leader, Abu Bakr al-Baghdadi, as Caliph.

Muslim theorists of the state argue that the essential Quranic principle of *Amr bil marouf wa nahy anil munkar* – "command good and forbid evil" – is the Islamic justification for the creation of an ideological state that is geared toward establishing the Islamic *sharia*. This principle is essentially drawn from the Quran [3:100, 3:104, and 9:710].

> You are the best of the nations raised up for (the benefit of) humanity; you enjoin what is right and forbid the wrong [Quran 3:110]

Since what is good and what is evil, they insist, is articulated in the *sharia*, in order for Muslims to fulfil the duty to 'enjoin the good' and forbid evil, Muslims must "establish the Islamic *sharia*." This is the standard justification for the Islamic state and was essentially articulated by a now-prominent medieval scholar, Ibn Taymiyyah. While one can always dispute whether the text of the Quran necessitates the creation of a state, the fact remains that a large segment of the Muslim population believes in it.

Given that many Muslims feel that Islam mandates political engagement as part of religious practice, Islam will continue to play a role in politics and public policy. In this brief essay, I want to depart from discussing the role of Islamic political movements in secular or Islamic states, such Saudi Arabia or Iran, and argue that there has emerged an idea of Islamic democracy in modern Muslim political discussions. In this brief article, written primarily to introduce the readership to the idea of a democratic Islamic polity, I identify and explore some key concepts that have salience to both Islamic religious political tradition and democratic theory.

The three Cs of Islamic Democracy

The key features of Islamic governance that I have found in Islamic sources – Quran and the Prophetic precedence (Sunnah), and contemporary Muslim discussions on the Islamic State – are Constitution, Consent, and Consultation. Muslims who seek to implement the *Sharia* are obliged to emulate the Prophet's precedence and, given the rather narrow definitions of *Sharia* and *Sunnah* that most Islamist operate with, there is no escape for them from the three key principles identified here. While these principles need to be explored and articulated in the specific socio-cultural context of different

Muslim societies, it is important to understand that they are essential.

Constitution

The compact, or constitution, of Medina that Prophet Muhammad adopted provides a very important occasion for the development of Islamic political theory. After Prophet Muhammad migrated from Mecca to Medina in 622 CE, he established the first Islamic state. For ten years, Prophet Muhammad was not only the leader of the emerging Muslim community in Arabia, but also the political head of the state of Medina. As the leader of Medina, Prophet Muhammad exercised jurisdiction over Muslims as well as non-Muslims. The legitimacy of his sovereignty over Medina was based on his status as the Prophet of Islam, as well as on the basis of the compact of Medina.

As Prophet of God, he had sovereignty over all Muslims by divine decree. But Muhammad did not rule over the non-Muslims of Medina because he was the messenger of Allah. He ruled over them by virtue of the compact that was signed by the *Muhajirun* (Muslim immigrants from Mecca), the Ansar (indigenous Muslims of Medina), and the *Yahud* (several Jewish tribes that lived in and around Medina). It is interesting to note that Jews were constitutional partners in the making of the first Islamic state.

The compact of Medina can be read as both a social contract and a constitution. A social contract, a model developed by English philosophers Thomas Hobbes and John Locke, is an imaginary agreement between people in the state of nature that leads to the establishment of a community or a State. In the state of nature people are free and are not obliged to follow any rules or laws. They are essentially sovereign individuals. However, through the social contract they surrender their individual sovereignty to a collective one and create a community or a State.

The second idea that the compact of Medina manifests is that of a constitution. In many ways, the constitution is the document that enshrines the conditions of the social contract upon which any society is founded. The compact of Medina clearly served a constitutional function, since it was the constitutive document for the first Islamic state. Thus, we can argue that the compact of Medina serves the dual function of a social contract and a constitution. Clearly the compact of Medina by itself cannot serve as a modern constitution. It would be quite inadequate, since it is a historically specific document and quite limited in its scope. However, it can serve as a guiding principle to be emulated, rather than a manual to be duplicated. Today, Muslims worldwide can emulate Prophet Muhammad and draw up their own constitutions, historically and temporally specific to their conditions.

Consent

An important principle of the Constitution of Medina was that Prophet Muhammad governed the city-state of Medina by virtue of the consent of its citizens. He was invited to govern, and his authority to govern was enshrined in the social contract. The constitution of Medina established the importance of consent and cooperation for governance.

The process of *bayah*, or the pledging of allegiance, was an important institution that sought to formalise the consent of the governed. In those days, when a ruler failed to gain the consent of the ruled through a formal and direct process of pledging of allegiance, the ruler's authority was not fully legitimised. This was an Arab custom that predates Islam, but, like many Arab customs, was incorporated within Islamic traditions. Just as Prophet Muhammad had done, the early Caliphs of Islam, too, practiced the process of *bayah* after rudimentary forms of electoral colleges had nominated the Caliph, in order to legitimise the authority of the Caliph. One does not need to stretch one's imagination too far to recognise that in polities that have millions rather than hundreds of citizens, the process of nomination followed by elections can serve as a necessary modernisation of the process of *bayah*. Replacing bayah with ballots makes the process of pledging allegiance simple and universal. Elections, therefore, are neither a departure from Islamic principles and traditions, nor inherently un-Islamic in any form.

The Quran, too, recognises the authority of those who have been chosen as leaders, and in a sense extends divine legitimacy to those who have legitimate authority.

> O you who believe! Obey Allah and obey the Messenger and those in authority from among you. [Quran 4:59]

Consultation

The third key principle of Islamic governance is consultation, or *Shura* in Arabic. This is a very widely known concept, and many Islamic scholars have advanced the Islamic concept of *Shura* as evidence for Islam's democratic credentials. Indeed, many scholars actually equate democracy with *Shura*.

> ...and consult them in affairs (of moment). Then, when thou hast taken a decision put thy trust in Allah. [Quran 3:159]

> [righteous are those] ...who conduct their affairs through [shura baynahum] mutual Consultation. [Quran 42:38]

Muslim scholars dispute whether the Quranic injunction for consultation is advisory or mandatory, but it nevertheless remains a divine sanction. Pro-democracy Muslims see it as necessary, and those who fear democratic freedoms and prefer authoritarianism interpret these injunctions as divine suggestions and not divine fiats. The Prophet himself left behind a very important tradition that emphasised the importance of collective and democratic decision making. He said that "the community of Muhammed will never agree upon error." Consultative governance, therefore, is the preferred form of governance in Islam, and any Muslim who chooses to stay true to his faith sources cannot but prefer a democratic structure over all others to realise the justice and wellbeing promised in Islamic sources.

Conclusion

There is much in Islamic sources and Islamic tradition that is favorable to making democracy the vehicle for delivering the products of Islamic governance, such as social justice, economic welfare, and religious freedoms. I am convinced that Islam is not a barrier to, but instead a facilitator of, democracy, justice, and tolerance in the Muslim world. That said, for that to happen, Muslims must revisit their sources and re-understand them without a bias against things that they erroneously label as Western. Democracy is inherent to Islamic values and Islamic historical experience.

References

Al-Raysuni, Ahmad. Al-Shura: *The Quranic Principle of Consultation* (London: International Institute of Islamic thought, 2011).

El Fadl, Khaled Abou, et al. *Islam and the Challenge of Democracy* (Princeton, NJ: Princeton University Press, 2004).

Esposito, John L., Mohammed A. Muqtedar Khan, and Jillian Schwedler. "Religion and Politics in the Middle East." *Understanding the Contemporary Middle East* (Boulder and London: Lynne Rienner Publishers, 2000).

Esposito, John L. and John O. Voll. *Islam and Democracy* (New York: Oxford University Press, 1996).

Haykal, M. H. The Life of Muhammad (trans.) Ismael R. Al Faruqi (Indianapolis: NAIT, 1988), pp. 180-83.

Khan, Muqtedar. "Shura and Democracy." *Ijtihad.Org*. http://www.ijtihad.org/shura.htm

Khan, M. A. Muqtedar. *Debating Moderate Islam: The Geopolitics of Islam and the West* (Salt Lake, Utah, University of Utah Press, 2007).

Khan, Muqtedar Khan. "Islam, Democracy and Islamism after the Counterrevolution in Egypt." *Middle East Policy* XXI.1 (2014): 75-86.

Khan, M. A. Muqtedar. "The Islamic States," in M. Hawkesworth and M. Kogan (Eds.), *Encyclopedia of Government and Politics*, (London: Routledge Press, 2003).

Siddiqui, A. H. *The Life of Muhammad* (Des Plaines, IL: Library of Islam, 1991).

Contributors

Haian Dukhan is a Ph.D. Candidate in the School of International Relations/Centre for Syrian Studies at the University of Saint Andrews. He holds a master's degree in International Development from the University of East Anglia.

Adel Elsayed Sparr is an M.Litt. (Master of Letters) graduate from the Middle East and Central Asian Security Studies program at the University of Saint Andrews. He also holds a B.A. in Arabic, as well as a B.Sc. in Political Science, both from Uppsala University. His research focuses on the State, international relations, the rule of law, legal pluralism, political theory, and foreign policy. He has been awarded the Wasenii scholarship and the Nissers scholarship for academic excellence. Mr. Elsayed Sparr currently works with the Consulate General of Sweden in Jerusalem. Author correspondence can be sent to adel.elsayedsparr@gmail.com.

Sinan Hawat is a London-based researcher specialising in complex emergencies and humanitarian aid. He obtained an M.Sc. in Development Management from the London School of Economics and Political Science, as well as postgraduate degree in Islamic and Humanities from the Institute of Ismaili Studies. He works as a researcher on the Middle East for a number of NGOs and charities.

Rana Khalaf is a research fellow with the Centre for Syrian Studies at the University of Saint Andrews. Her current research focuses on conflict, governance, civil-society, activism, youth, social protection, and neoliberal peace; it geographically concentrates on the non-government controlled parts of Syria. Her papers 'Governance without Government in Syria: Civil-Society and State-Building during Conflict' and 'Activism in Difficult Times – Civil Society in Syria (2011-2014)' cut new grounds in academia. They tackle local dynamics during the conflict itself. These remain rather unknown and misunderstood. For more information, visit lb.linkedin.com/in/ranakhalaf.

Joseph J. Kaminski is Associate Professor in the Faculty of Social and Political Sciences at the International University of Sarajevo, in Bosnia and Herzegovina. He holds a Ph.D. in Political Science from Purdue University, as well as an M.A. in Political Science from City University New York. His primary research interests are in political theory/political philosophy and comparative politics, with a regional focus on the Muslim World. He is also interested in political development and organizational management theory. He can be contacted at jkaminski@ius.edu.ba.

M.A. Muqtedar Khan is Associate Professor in the department of Political Science and International Relations at the University of Delaware and a Fellow of the Institute for Social Policy and Understanding. His website is www.ijtihad.org and his academic depository is https://udel.academia.edu/MuqtedarKhan.

Maximilian Laktisch is a researcher at the Austrian Study Centre for Peace and Conflict Resolution. He has published about conflict theory, peacebuilding, Political Islam, and the Middle East. Maximilian has edited 'Political Power Reconsidered: State Power and Civic Activism between Legitimacy and Violence' (Lit 2014). He has published in various journals like the Peace Studies Journal, as well as in Online Information Networks like Shabka and The Medes. He can be contacted at laktisch@aspr.ac.uk and followed at his Academia.edu profile.

Juan A. Macías-Amoretti is a Senior Lecturer in Arabic and Islamic Studies at the University of Granada, a Research Fellow in Contemporary Arab Studies at UGR, and a Research Associate Fellow at the Jacques Berque Centre in Rabat. His areas of research include political Islam and contemporary Arab political thought.

Mohammed Nuruzzaman is Associate Professor of International Relations at the Gulf University for Science and Technology, Kuwait. His primary areas of teaching and research interests are international relations theories, global political economy, traditional and non-traditional security studies, great powers in the global order, and international relations of the Middle East. He has published in leading international peer-reviewed journals, including International Studies Perspectives, Cooperation and Conflict, New Global Studies, Journal of Contemporary Asia, International Studies, Journal of Asian and African Studies, Strategic Analysis, Global Change, and Peace & Security.

Note on Indexing

E-IR's publications do not feature indexes due to the prohibitive costs of assembling them. However, if you are reading this book in paperback and want to find a particular word or phrase you can do so by downloading a free e-book version of this publication in PDF from the E-IR website.

When downloaded, open the PDF on your computer in any standard PDF reader such as Adobe Acrobat Reader (pc) or Preview (mac) and enter your search terms in the search box. You can then navigate through the search results and find what you are looking for. In practice, this method can prove much more targeted and effective than consulting an index.

If you are using apps such as iBooks or Kindle to read our e-books, you should also find word search functionality in those.

You can find all of our e-books at: http://www.e-ir.info/publications

www.ingramcontent.com/pod-product-compliance
Lightning Source LLC
Chambersburg PA
CBHW071023080526
44587CB00015B/2472